YORKSI WOLDS WANDERINGS

Revised second edition

A guide to walking, cycling
and touring in the Yorkshire Wolds
by
David F. Walford.

Illustrations
by Peter Steel
Route Maps and
Additional Illustrations
by David F Walford.

SANTONA PUBLICATIONS
HULL
2003

Yorkshire Wolds Wanderings
First Published 1997
Second Edition 2003

Front Cover Illustration
Drewton Dale, South Cave.
Back Cover Illustration
All Saints Church
Brantingham Dale.
Photos by Steve Flint.

British Library Cataloguing-in-Publication Data.
A Catalogue record for this book is available from the British Library
Copyright © 2003 by **David F. Walford.**
First Published in 1997
This edition published 2003 by Santona Publications, Rydal Mount, 224,
Marlborough Avenue, Hull HU5 3LE

Printed and bound by Fisk Printers, Hull.

ISBN 0 9538448 6 2

Also by the same Author;
Yorkshire Railway Rambles Vol. 1 North & East
It Was To Be The Big One

The Spirit of Santona
Onward to the Horizon

SANTONA PUBLICATIONS
HULL

Foreword

Yorkshire Wolds Wanderings has been written by East Yorkshireman David F. Walford, who has been striding over these chalk hills ever since he could walk. Through these pages he takes you on a descriptive tour of many of his favourite locations; from around Brigg, on the northern Lincolnshire Wolds, up through the very heart of East Yorkshire to Flamborough Head and along the coast to Scarborough in North Yorkshire. He has used his special knowledge of rambling and transport history, combined with a general history of the area, to create this wonderful insight into the still relatively undiscovered Yorkshire Wolds.

Together with the interesting and well described walks and rambles which will help you uncover the secrets of the area, he provides valuable advice about map reading and the necessary procedures you should follow to ensure full enjoyment of your days in the countryside.

Throughout the book, a wealth of graphic information about routes and pathways is provided by numerous detailed maps all drawn by David himself. As well as the recommended routes, the maps also show places of special interest which deserve a visit. Alternative routes are also suggested, giving differing lengths of walks, from short hour-long rambles to full day treks and cycle rides.

David has used Hull artist Peter Steel to beautifully illustrate many of the local landscapes and townscapes. To recreate the bygone scenes, Peter drew his inspiration from old photographs and paintings as well as from the landscape itself. Pictures of historic buildings that have long since disappeared under the demolition hammer are all creatively combined with numerous nature and wildlife studies.

Yorkshire Wolds Wanderings, with its rich blend of information, maps, history, walks and sketches, will inspire ramblers, cyclists, historians and countryside lovers everywhere to explore and gain much pleasure from this unspoilt part of the English countryside.

YORKSHIRE WOLDS WANDERINGS

Contents

Acknowledgements

With special thanks to my wife Sarah, also to the late Raymond Flint, to Joan Flint, Steve Flint, and to Peter Steel for their encouragement and assistance in the preparation of this book.

David F. Walford.

Introduction

As a very keen walker, the Yorkshire Wolds gave me my earliest experiences of country walking and although I am now often to be seen tackling far greater challenges high up in the Scottish Mountains, the much undervalued Yorkshire Wolds still have a very special appeal to me.

My aim with this book is to set you off on an exploration of the many unspoilt grassy dales and villages throughout the beautiful Wolds. It will guide you on both long and short countryside rambles, look back at sites of deserted settlements and long lost great houses and review the many transport routes that have come and gone over the years.

Hull artist Peter Steel has ably illustrated the book with his pencil sketches of many of the prominent buildings and landmarks that feature in the Yorkshire Wolds. Some views are modern, such as the world beating suspension bridge across the Humber, others are period pieces capturing the Wolds at the turn of the last century. A time, long before the invasion of the motor car, when horse's hooves clopped along rough tracks and steam railway locomotives powered trains over (and through) the high chalk hills.

I will start by reviewing the area around the Humber Bridge and Hessle foreshore on the north bank and even venture over to Barton upon Humber, South Ferriby and Brigg amidst the Lincolnshire Wolds. The journey will then progress northwards, looking at the dales around South Cave, Brantingham, Welton and up to Skidby. Next we will consider the Beverley area with special mention of the Hudson Way, then, still travelling northwards, we will venture into the heart of the Wolds to uncover Warter, Millington Pasture and Huggate and the higher dales around Wharram, Thixendale and Burdale.

Finally, as we journey eastwards towards the coast and the cliffs at Flamborough Head, we will take a peep at the beautiful country houses of Sledmere, Burton Agnes and Sewerby and conclude the rambles with a trek northwards to Bempton, Filey Brigg and Scarborough.

I hope with this book that you too will share in the joy, tranquillity and inspiration the Yorkshire Wolds have given me for many, many years.

David F. Walford.

List of Walks

List of Illustrations

Chapter 1

THE YORKSHIRE WOLDS - A BRIEF PREAMBLE.

The Yorkshire Wolds are formed from the most northerly deposits of chalk in the British Isles. The dramatic cliffs of Flamborough Head, jutting majestically out from the East Yorkshire coastline, mark the beginning of these chalk uplands. Turning away from the North Sea, they sweep inland in a broad arc cutting across the heart of East Yorkshire, firstly in a westwardly direction then southerly until they meet the banks of the River Humber at Ferriby, 12km west of the city of Kingston upon Hull. The chalk deposits then stretch southwards, forming the Lincolnshire Wolds before spreading both south and west through England to the North and South Downs and into Kent, meeting the sea again to create the glorious White Cliffs of Dover. To the west, a spur drives over to the barren hills of Salisbury Plain in Wiltshire.

Any visitor to the Yorkshire Wolds will know they have a very unique character about them. Still, calm, somehow unhurried by the twenty first century thundering past. The porous geology of the chalk rules that water will soak through very quickly resulting in mile after mile of dry valleys and thinly covered grass heath. Unique characteristics that give all chalk dales throughout the country a very similar appearance.

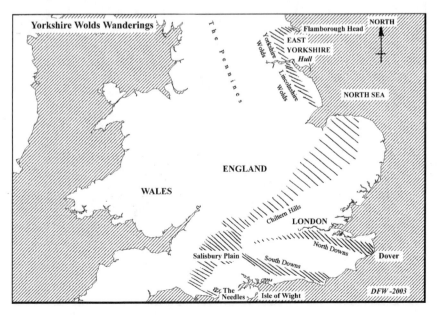

13

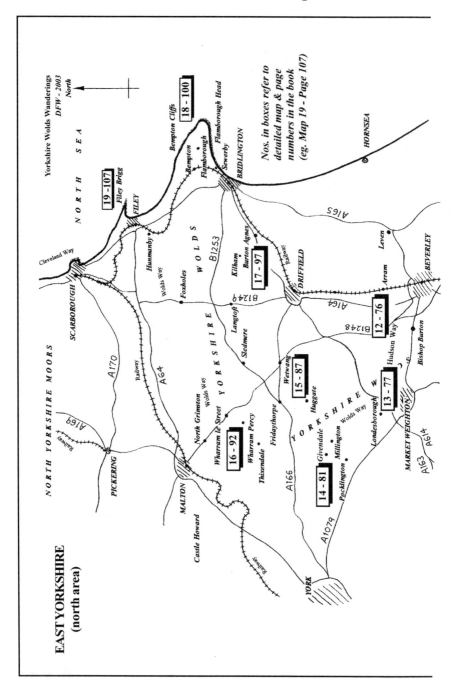

EAST YORKSHIRE
(north area)

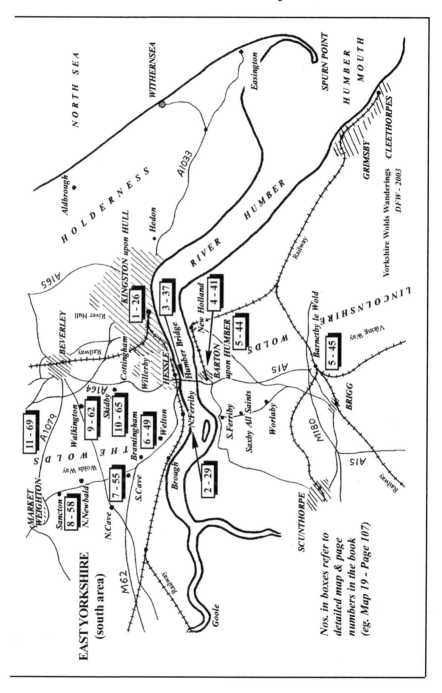

EAST YORKSHIRE (south area)

Nos. in boxes refer to detailed map & page numbers in the book (eg. Map 19 - Page 107)

Yorkshire Wolds Wanderings
DFW - 2003

Yorkshire Wolds Wanderings

Always regarded as the largest traditional county in England, Yorkshire extends from County Durham and the river Tees in the north, down to the river Humber. This broad stretch of water has long served to isolate the Lincolnshire 'Yellow Bellies' from the 'Yorkshire Tykes'. In the west, the Pennines form the natural border and boundary with several other counties, the 'Red Rose County' of Lancashire being the most prominent.

Over the past thirty years, the Boundary Commission has had a few very unwelcome attempts at removing various chunks of the County of Yorkshire. The most acrimonious, of course, being the formation in 1974 of the County of Humberside. At the demands of its population, after just 22 years of uncomfortable existence, The County of Humberside crumbled and finally disappeared on 1st April 1996 and the East Riding made a much exalted and spirited return to the map of Yorkshire.

Outside the county, there is a definite lack of knowledge and awareness of the natural wonders that form the Yorkshire Wolds and of the interesting towns and villages that make up the East Riding, not forgetting, of course, the much revived city of Kingston upon Hull. The full page maps on the previous pages give you all the principal towns, rivers and transport links in the areas covered by this book.

The Wolds reach a maximum height above sea level of 246m (807 feet). To the east their height gently drops until meeting the Plain of Holderness, formed principally of boulder clay soil, much of which is drained by the River Hull. The southern border is marked by the River Humber, the largest river estuary in the country said to drain away no less than one fifth of all rain water in England. The northern and western slopes of the Yorkshire Wolds are steep escarpments which drop sharply down to the Vale of Pickering and the Vale of York, to be drained by the rivers Derwent and Ouse, which themselves flow into the Humber.

Over the centuries many people have settled in this part of England, enriching the history of the area and leaving many teasing clues about their ways of life. A number of Roman roads cross the area, the main one being Ermine Street. This main artery from Lincoln to York crossed the River Humber by a ford south of the Roman settlement at Petuaria, where Brough is now located on the north bank. This suggests that, without the modern day dredging of the river-bed and the countless number of man-made rain water drains and dykes, river levels were quite possibly much shallower some two thousand years ago.

The Yorkshire Wolds - A Brief Preamble

The Romans were followed by the Saxons, the Viking invaders and then the Danes who settled, leaving many traces of their existence in East Yorkshire. Indeed the origins of many place names in this area can be traced back to this period in our history. A close look at the Ordnance Survey maps covering East Yorkshire reveals a wealth of former village sites suggesting many changes in culture and farming methods over the centuries. And from later centuries, numerous large country houses with their parkland covering hundreds of acres can be located, some still standing and occupied, others just a distant memory.

The last hundred years or so has seen the most changes to the Wolds since the Ice Age. The industrial revolution brought many significant changes to the area and contributed to the rising importance and rapid growth of the ancient port of Hull. In particular, the coming of the railways bringing coal and food and raw materials for new industries as well as goods for export. Further expansion of the railway network opened up many of the farming areas and enabled them to gain access to the market towns of Driffield, Beverley and Market Weighton.

In the 20th century it was the turn of the roads and motorways to further open up this corner of England. And, after years of planning, the completion of the Humber Bridge, the World's longest single span crossing at the time it was opened.

Whether you are walking, cycling or travelling by car, it makes good sense to always plan your visit beforehand and to be conversant with basic map-reading skills. It is also important to be aware of established common sense rules when visiting the countryside.

A good understanding of maps and knowledge of the Country Code will enhance your enjoyment whilst wandering around the Yorkshire Wolds. The next chapter contains valuable help, advice and assistance about these aspects.

Chapter 2

PLANNING YOUR WALKS.

If you intend to leave the confines of your transport and venture deeper into the countryside please make yourself aware of the following guidelines, particularly as much of the area is farmed and would suffer from intruders who do not display respect for the countryside.

Follow the Country Code, in particular, keep to public rights of way. If you take your dog it must be under full control at all times. Have a spare plastic bag with you so that you can take all of your litter home. If you find a gate shut, please check after you have passed through, that it is snecked shut properly. Unattended farm machinery may look very interesting to the children but do not let them tamper with it, it could be damaged or worse, could cause a serious injury. If you are on a cycle or horseback, understand the difference between footpaths and bridleways (see below) and avoid causing yourself, as well as other visitors, inconvenience and difficulties.

The maps in this book are intended as general guides only and you should seek out your route or circular path using only public rights of way as marked on OS maps. Every attempt is made to ensure that the information is correct at the time of going to press, but always please take note of any footpath diversion instructions that are made from time to time.

The paths and tracks marked on the maps contained in this book is no absolute guarantee of the existence of a public right of way as many have been recorded from personal knowledge. Please also note that some private roads are only marked to assist you to identify your exact position. If you are in any doubt about a right of way, then before you set out, you can contact the local Highways Department who will have up to date information.

Public rights of way are generally quite well signposted, though it is always advisable to have the appropriate Ordnance Survey map with you. The numbers of the Landranger Series of OS maps that cover this area are: 100 and 101 for the North Wolds, 106 and 107 for the remainder of the Wolds and Holderness, and No. 112 to guide you over the Humber Bridge and into the northern Lincolnshire Wolds. The OS Landranger Series are the most commonly used, being all purpose maps, with a scale of 1:50,000 (1.25 inches to the mile). For more detailed maps at a scale of

Planning Your Walks

1:25,000 (2.5 inches to the mile), seek out the OS Pathfinder Series. Over the past few years the Ordnance Survey has reproduced the Pathfinder series as Explorer Maps to the same scale. Although costing a little more than the Landranger series, for the enthusiastic walker or cyclist they are of immense value and contain additional tourist information. The numbers to look out for are; 300 and 301 for the northern Wolds, 294 and 293 for the central and southern Wolds, 295 and 292 for Holderness and the coast. Northern Lincolnshire is shown on sheet numbers 281 and 284. The following diagram confirms all the map numbers.

There are three main types of right of way you can follow into the countryside; Footpaths, Bridleways and Green Lanes (tracks or unsurfaced roads used as a public right of way). By simple definition; on a footpath you can only walk and it will be around 1.2m to 1.5m wide. A bridleway is open to walkers, cyclists and horse riders. It is usually 3m wide and will have gates instead of styles to cross walls or hedges. A track or green lane is technically open to all forms of transport, but should still be treated with utmost respect. In recent years the 4 wheel drive vehicle has become fashionable, and these machines can create terrible damage to the fragile countryside if used carelessly. These ancient green lanes were created in an age when the most powerful force known to man was a horse - the Range Rover was yet to be born!

If you are unfamiliar with map reading, these few tips should help. Maps nearly always position north at the top, if possible face north yourself to read the map when you are on your rambles. If you are unsure which direction you are facing, then use a compass to establish north and face that way.

View the surrounding countryside and refer to the map to get your 'bearings' and a feel for the area. For example, pinpoint a landmark, such as a church, on the map then locate it in the landscape. Likewise, if you're standing next to farm buildings with a lane going off to the right, (east), find the position on the map then trace the route of the path out. After studying a few views with a map in your hands you will soon learn how to identify your location and the surrounding landscape. Practical use such as this is the best way to learn how to read a map.

In this book all distances are in metres and kilometres. If you are more at home with feet and miles remember the simple conversions to help you. One metre is 3.2808 feet, so a quick conversion is one metre to just over

Index to Ordnance Survey Maps
Landranger & Explorer(in brackets)

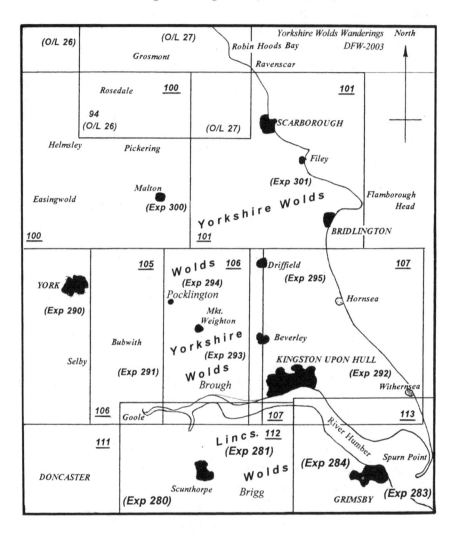

Map Index courtesy Ordnance Survey
© Crown copyright (2003)

three feet. One kilometre is 0.625 miles, thus 8 kilometres (8km), are equal to 5 miles. As a further help the grid lines on the OS maps divides the country into one square kilometres, thereby giving you a quick guide to the distance between places by counting the grid lines crossed.

Another useful skill is to learn how to take a grid reference. At the bottom of the key on all OS maps, a simple example is given how to find any location on a map using a six number grid reference. Remember the 'Easting' comes first (read horizontally along the bottom of the map), and the 'Northing' second (read vertically up the side of the map). A grid reference number is quoted in the 'Fact File' accompanying each walk, giving you the exact start and finish point.

If you have the misfortune to have an accident in the countryside, giving the emergency services a grid reference for the casualty may save vital minutes in a rescue situation, when you are not familiar with road and place names, or you are on a bleak moorland area. Keep testing yourself and your friends, it is a very simple system to learn, but can be very important.

When you get back home many enjoyable hours can be spent re-tracing your route taken that day and planning a course for the next day. You will

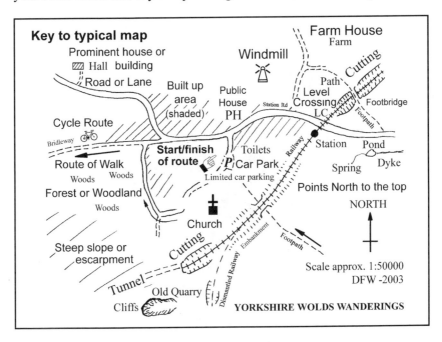

also soon get a feel for distances and the type of terrain; flat, gentle slopes, very steep grassy climb, etc. If you want to progress to backpacking in the wilds of Scotland, this is the best way to learn your map reading skills beforehand.

When you are going on even a short walk, it is always wise to be suitably clothed. A stout pair of shoes or boots and a waterproof coat are really the minimum essentials. Use a rucksack rather than a hand held bag to carry your belongings safely, with, of course, your OS maps. Even on The Wolds it is a good idea to always have a whistle in your rucksack and some spare food and clothes.

If you are tackling the Wolds on your bike be sure to wear the correct cycling gear including that most important helmet. Have a bright coloured jacket on or bright panniers at the back, so that you really stand out to traffic behind you. Keep the water bottles filled and check your machine over before and after every journey, especially if you have been off road. That's enough of the theory, let's now start our wanderings around the Wolds on foot, cycle or by car. Have fun!

Lund Village Pump

Chapter 3

AROUND THE HUMBER BRIDGE

Walk 1. HESSLE FORESHORE to HULL CITY CENTRE.

Situated 8km west of Hull city centre, the town of Hessle has grown over many years. The elegant spire of All Saints Church looks down on a mixture of houses and shops spreading out from the Square (though Hessle Square is a relatively modern feature of this town dating from the 1920s). From a transport point of view Hessle was quite a significant centre. The road out of Hull to the west ran through the town centre and a Humber ferry originally sailed from Hessle Haven across to Barton upon Humber, hence the 'Ferry Boat Inn' at the corner of Livingstone Road. This road, incidentally, takes its name from the former Livingstone's shipbuilding yard located on the west bank of the haven. Henry Scarr's yard, another shipbuilding firm which later became Richard Dunstons, was situated on the east bank. Like the ferry, both shipyards have now vanished and the many skilled and dedicated craftsmen who once built ships by the hundred have moved on too.

With the building of the Hull and Selby Railway in 1840 many large houses were built around the new station at Hessle. Wealthy merchants approved of being able to live outside the town of Hull and commute daily by the railway to work. This accounts too, for many of the Victorian residential developments in the 19th century at Brough, North Ferriby and Hessle itself. Large three and four storey houses, whose owners would have employed servants to attend the needs of the household, were built within walking distance of the railway stations.

To walkers and ramblers, Hessle is the official start/finish of The Wolds Way long distance footpath. This is a trek of 127km (79 miles) of country walking over the full length of these chalk hills ending at Filey Brigg. The complete route is well documented in several books still in print and makes an ideal starter for those wanting to tackle more challenging walks.

With the opening of the World record-breaking Humber Bridge, just west of Hessle, a large country park and public facilities were developed. Part of the country park was formed over what was the original Hessle Golf Club course, but most of it was developed around an area known locally as 'Little Switzerland', created from the remains of a series of large chalk quarries that were worked for many years. The quarries had

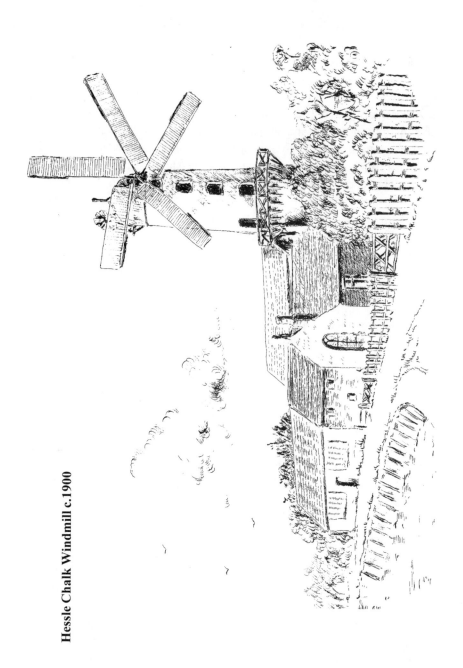

Hessle Chalk Windmill c.1900

their own railway system to transport the chalk down to Hessle foreshore where a series of jetties were built for final dispatch by boat. Some of the chalk was also sent out by rail along the adjacent mainline.

The large black structure close to the north tower of the Humber Bridge was once a five-sailed wind mill used for grinding the chalk on site. The sketch in this book is inspired by an original water colour painting of the mill shown working around the turn of the previous century.

With its large car parks and public facilities the Humber Bridge Country Park makes an excellent base for a few hours of rambling. The car parks have their access on Ferriby Road, well sign posted from the A63 trunk road and from the A15 Humber Bridge road. Further car parks are located on the Hessle foreshore, off Livingstone Road, adjacent to the north tower foundations of the bridge.

Looking at the map you will see that public footpaths lead both easterly along the river bank into the heart of Hull and the mouth of the River Hull, and westerly along to North Ferriby and Brough Haven.

The path into Hull City centre is about 8km long (so would take around two hours). Throughout most of its length it clings to the river bank. Starting on Hessle foreshore in the shadow of the Humber Bridge north tower, it takes you past the sites of the old shipyards and over Hessle Haven by a new road bridge next to the A63 trunk road. You soon return to the river bank and continue walking eastward.

The path, now squeezed between the new trunk road and the river bank, brings you to the old St. Andrew's fish dock (now a retail park with large car parks), then past the present fish docks; William Wright Dock and the larger Albert Dock.

This section of the walk is very interesting as you are now sandwiched between the dock storage warehouses and the river. The remains of the old riverside quay (destroyed by enemy action in the last war) are visible here. Now the route climbs a series of steps to follow the footpath over the last hundred metres of warehouses on a gantry along the rooftops of the sheds.

This splendid and unusual elevated position gives you an excellent panoramic view of the river and the city skyline. A good idea here, is to have a pair of binoculars handy to help you absorb the splendid views in greater detail. Dropping down to ground level again and signposts clearly guide you over the lock gates and out of the dock estate. Turning eastward

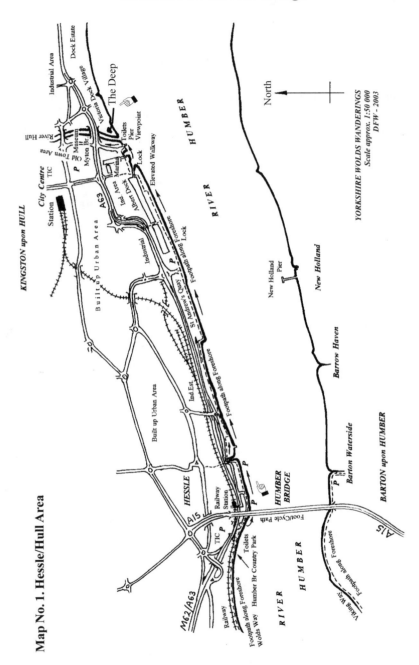

Map No. 1. Hessle/Hull Area

to the right, you are now near the city centre and the original town docks (now a marina). Another set of lock gates are then crossed and you enter the old town area of the city.

The first railway station to open in Hull was located here, just to the west of Humber Dock. This dock, along with Railway Dock, is now enjoying a vibrant new life as a busy marina, one of the best equipped marinas on the east coast of Britain in fact. The old Corporation pier exists in reduced form as a view point for the river, marking the spot where the last ferries made their frequent crossing to New Holland pier at the south side of the river.

Plenty of public facilities are located around the pier area as well as in the city centre. Tourist Information offices are to be found in Victoria Square and the central library in Albion Street. A train or bus ride, departing

Fact File: Hessle Foreshore to Hull City Centre

Start/Finish: Hessle Foreshore to Hull Corporation Pier. Grid refs: TA 024253/TA 100282. A flat riverbank walk, (2 sets of steps - Albert Dock).
Location: Cliff Road, nr. Humber Br. car parks/Queen St., Nelson St. old town area of Hull.
Max. length of main walk: (one way): 9km (5.5 miles), typical time 3 hours.
Length of shorter walk: (St Andrew's Quay & return): 6km (4 miles), 1.5 hours.
OS maps: Landranger 107, Pathfinder 696, (TA 02/12), Explorer 293.
Refreshments: Plenty of choice at Humber Br. & Hull centre.
Other Information: A flat walk all along the river bank, good views of City from elevated position on shed roofs at Albert Dock. Museums in High St., Hull. Transport back to start point. Take care at lock gates when leaving Dock Estate. Frequent bus and train service: Hull, Ferensway to Hessle.
Tourist Information: Offices at Humber Bridge (01482) 640852 & Victoria Square, Hull. Tel: (01482) 223559.

from Paragon Station on Ferensway, returns you to Hessle and your transport home.

A new footbridge, (including cycleway) now crosses the River Hull to the south of the tidal barrier and close to the mouth of the river. This links the old town area with the exciting new Submarium called The Deep. This strikingly shaped wedge building located where the River Hull meets the River Humber, is one of the most successful Millennium projects in the country. In its first year of operation it attracted almost one million visitors from all over the world and should be on your list of places to visit in the city centre. The new bridge also links with footpaths along the river front and Victoria Dock Village.

Walk 2: HESSLE FORESHORE to WELTON and BROUGH.

Walking from the Humber Bridge heading west, you have a 4km walk to reach Ferriby Foreshore and a further 5km walk to Brough Haven. Both North Ferriby and Brough are large villages with railway stations, so return to Hessle is possible by public transport if you only wish to walk one way. Again you start from the foreshore by the north tower of the Humber Bridge. The path clings to the waters edge and it was along this stretch of foreshore that significant archaeological finds have been made. The thick mud of the Humber banks at North Ferriby acted as a preservative for a number of ancient timber boats discovered earlier last century. The first, a Bronze Age boat was found in 1937, followed by a second in 1940. A third, found in 1963, is now on permanent display in Hull's Archaeology museum. Many Roman coins and pottery have also been located in this area over the years.

The short route finishes here for return to Hessle via the railway station, however, if you want to extend your walk, various paths head north away from the river. At Long Plantation to the west of Ferriby a path will take you north, over the railway to Melton Hill, then on to Welton past a very large working quarry to the north. Take great care crossing the A63 trunk road which is very busy at this point being the main artery road in and out of Hull. If you have children with you it is worth taking the short detour west to use the footbridge. A major new scheme to rebuild this section of highway, separating the through traffic onto flyovers should commence in the near future. Care should also be taken crossing Great Gutter Lane, as

Around the Humber Bridge

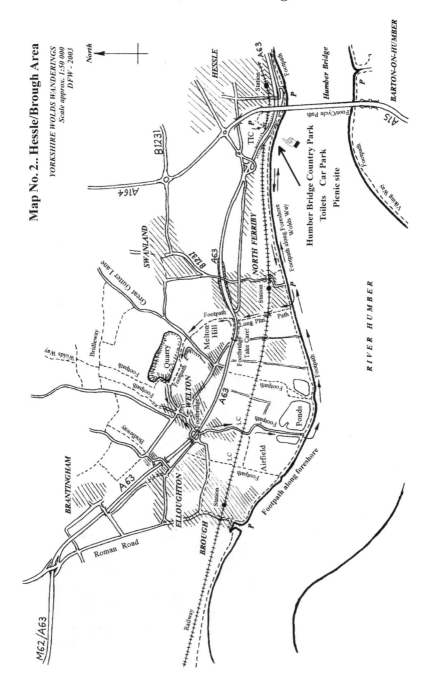

Map No. 2.. Hessle/Brough Area

YORKSHIRE WOLDS WANDERINGS
Scale approx. 1:50 000
DFW - 2003

North

HESSLE

Station

A63

Footpath

Humber Bridge

BARTON-ON-HUMBER

Foot/Cycle Path

A15

TIC

P

Humber Bridge Country Park
Toilets   Car Park
Picnic site

Footpath along Foreshore
Wolds Way

Footpath

Viking Way

B1231

A164

SWANLAND

B1231

A63

NORTH FERRIBY

Station

P

RIVER HUMBER

Great Gutter Lane

Footpath

Melton
Hill

Bridleway

Wolds Way

Quarry

Footpath

Footpath

WELTON

Footbridge

Long Plan

Footbridge
Take Care!

Path

Footpath

Ponds

Footpath

Footpath

BRANTINGHAM

A63

Bridleway

ELLOUGHTON

A63

LC

LC

Airfield

Footpath

Footpath along foreshore

Station

P

BROUGH

Roman   Road

Railway

M62/A63

29

St Helens Church, Welton

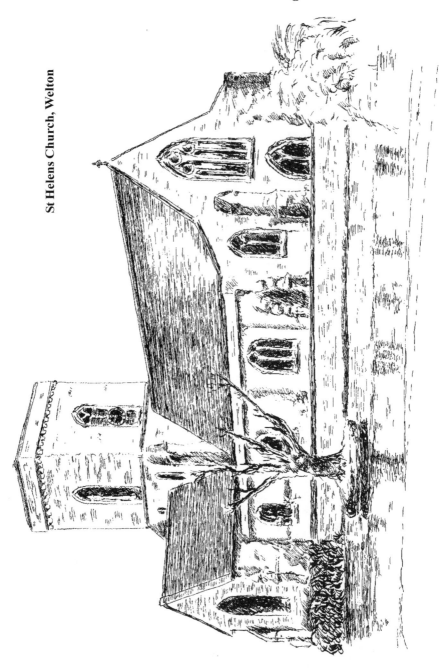

this can also be a fast road at the side of the quarries. Melton Hill was the location for Welton House, the large county mansion built for the Raikes family in the 19th century. Though demolished in 1953, a substantial mausoleum built in 1818 for the family still stands in the woods higher up Welton Dale.

After passing the large quarries you enter Welton village from the north side, walking down to the delightful stream that bubbles southwards to the village pond, next to the church of St Helen's. A few paces further is the village pub, The Green Dragon. Continuing further south a footbridge enables you to re-cross the always busy A63 in safety. Head back along Common Lane passing the many glasshouses, then over the railway crossing and down to the river. To your right is an airfield at the side of the huge British Aerospace factory.

This was one of the first aeroplane factories in the country, founded by Robert Blackburn in 1916 as an extension to his new factory in Leeds. With easy access to the Humber and adjacent flat land for an airfield, this site was chosen for the building of both aeroplanes and seaplanes. The close proximity of the Leeds to Hull railway for supplies was another factor. Over the years it has been associated with many famous aircraft; The Blackburn Beverley, The Buccaneer, The Hawk, and it is still the largest single source of employment in the area.

The return to Hessle from the airfield is approximately 8km eastward along the waters edge via North Ferriby (see overleaf for Factfile).

Fact File: Hessle to Welton and Brough Area Walks

Start/Finish: Hessle Foreshore and/or Humber Bridge car parks. Grid Ref: TA 024253

Max. length of main walk: 19km (12 miles), typical time: 5 hours. Generally flat easy walking.

Length of shorter ramble to North Ferriby only: 8km (5 miles), time: 1.5 hours.

OS maps: Landranger 106, Pathfinder 695 & 696, (SE 82/92, TA 02/12), Explorer 293

Bus & Train service: Hessle, North Ferriby & Brough.

Refreshments: Humber Br. & Pubs/shops at each village centre.

Other Information: Cross A63 & Great Gutter Lane with care!

Tourist Information: Office at Humber Bridge car park off Ferriby Road, Tel: (01482) 640852.

General: A pleasant river walk with gentle slopes around Welton. The river walk is not suitable for cycles.

Walk 3: HUMBER BRIDGE CIRCULAR.

It should go without saying that some time should be spent marvelling at the magnificence of the Humber Bridge. The statistics are quite mind blowing for the World's longest span bridge when opened in 1981 by Her Majesty The Queen on the 17th July.

The River Humber has always been a natural boundary across north east England. Much wider than most river estuaries it has been the location for many elaborate schemes to tunnel under, or bridge over, its tidal waters. Most historians accept that the Romans built a ford to cross the river between Brough on the north bank and Winteringham, near South Ferriby on the Lincolnshire side, thus continuing Ermine Street northwards to York and beyond. It is possible that a boat would have to be used even at low tide to cross the deeper north channel in the river bed, but it is clear that without the extensive land drainage schemes that have been developed over the past centuries, the water level would have been much lower at low tide.

Paddle Steamer Wingfield Castle c.1960

Records show that various ferries were crossing the Humber by the late 18th century. By that time the Hessle to Barton and Hull to Barton boats had taken the majority of the trade. As the Port of Kingston upon Hull developed, so demands grew for a crossing taking passengers and goods from the heart of the port by a more direct route southwards. A new ferry crossing was established between New Holland pier and Hull Corporation pier in 1832. This route soon established its position as the main ferry crossing. The developing railway companies naturally took an active interest in controlling a ferry crossing to connect passengers with their developing rail network and in 1845 the Hull to New Holland service (being the most lucrative crossing) was taken over by the Great Grimsby and Sheffield Junction Railway. This company built a branch line on the south bank to connect the ferry traffic with their main railway line from Grimsby to Gainsborough. This railway company later became part of the larger Manchester, Sheffield and Lincolnshire Railway, and as such proved a threat to the North Eastern Railway company that dominated the north bank of the Humber. Against the competition, the other ferry routes steadily fell into decline, leaving the Hull to New Holland crossing to develop unchallenged.

Over the years the ferry boats were steadily improved to suit this difficult crossing and the types of trade that developed. The most notorious difficulty was the shallow nature of the river, with its shifting mud banks and very fast flowing currents. One part of the tide would see the shallow draught, flat bottomed ferry boats sailing well down the river before steaming back up along the opposite shore line, thereby keeping to the deep water channel.

A careless manoeuvre would have the ferry stuck fast on a mud bank awaiting the incoming tide to release its impatient passengers.

Not surprisingly the 'Railway Mania' periods of the 19th century brought various proposals to cross the river with a permanent railway link, including a scheme for a 2km long viaduct from Hessle to Barton. The first serious plan that was laid before Parliament was for a tunnel under the river at a cost of almost one million pounds.

In 1872 the Bill promoted by The Hull, South and West Junction Railway Company was actually passed by the House of Commons and only faulted on reaching the House of Lords who doubted the technical abilities of the Victorian engineers to tunnel under the river and the credibility of the one million pound price tag.

The Humber Bridge

Maybe it is a pity that the same House of Lords saw no such possible troubles for engineers building the now defunct Ennerdale road tunnel under the River Hull! They probably assumed that if Marc and Isumbard Brunel were capable of tunnelling under the much wider River Thames back in 1825, then almost two centuries on, engineers would be rather more experienced to enable them to cut and backfill a short tunnel 10km upstream from the Humber!

However, I digress. It was in the 1930s that serious plans were again put forward to cross the Humber, this time by a multispan girder bridge, carrying not a railway but a road. In 1931 the plans faltered with the collapse of the MacDonald government and the economical crisis of the thirties. The proposals were finally lost with the outbreak of war and improvements that were made to the ferry service.

These improvements included modifications to the piers at Hull and New Holland, allowing motor vehicles to drive onto the ferry boats instead of being lifted on by crane.

It was to be the 1960s before new plans were drawn up for a single span suspension bridge. The design was to be similar to the Severn Bridge then under construction, following the opening of the Fourth Road Bridge in 1964. The towers were to be of reinforced concrete design, while the road carrying deck sections would be of a box girder construction. This time the economic and political climate was rather different and the Minister of Transport of that period, Mrs. Barbara Castle, gave the go ahead for the Humber Bridge project in 1966.

However, it was not until late in 1972 that Hessle foreshore became a hive of activity when preparations began for work to start in earnest early in 1973. Eventually, the north bank bridge tower rose majestically to 155.5m above the pier foundations located at the high water mark. Whilst simultaneously, just to the north of the main railway line out of Hull, the huge cable anchorage took shape.

A 500m long jetty gave access from the Barton foreshore to the foundations of the south tower. Unlike the north tower (built straight on to the hard chalk), the south tower was to give considerable problems requiring caissons to be sunk 30m below the Humber mud to find a solid base. The optimistic programme had the opening date for 1976/77. Through a combination of industrial disputes and design problems (particularly with the south tower foundations) this programme drifted into 1981 when the

Around the Humber Bridge

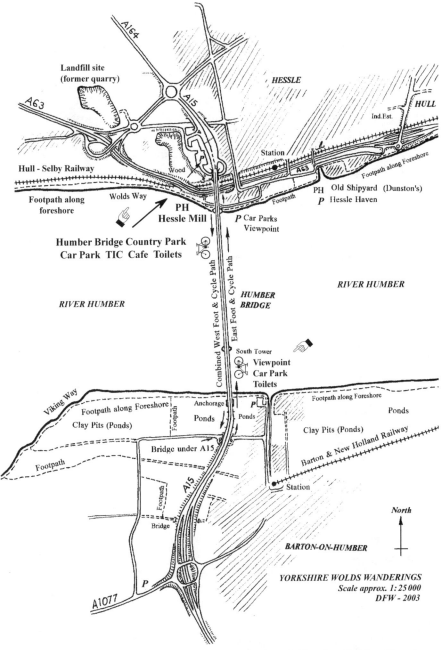

Map No. 3. Humber Bridge Circular

first toll paying vehicles finally crossed the river on 24th June. That day also witnessed the last ever ferry crossing from New Holland Pier to Corporation Pier by the 'Farringford', a diesel powered paddle vessel.

The official opening of the bridge was carried by Her Majesty the Queen on the 17th July 1981. What ever one thinks about the logic of building the Humber Bridge, the statistics are exceptional. The world-beating centre span (when it was built) is 1,410m between the towers, with overall length of the bridge between the two anchorages 2,220m. The 155.5m high towers lift the road deck over 30m clear of the high water mark. Almost half a million tonnes of concrete went into the construction of the bridge, along with 16,500 tonnes of steel in the decking and 71,000km of wire, spun to form the main cables, which themselves weigh a mighty 11,000 tonnes.

The region, having lived with the bridge for almost a quarter of a century, still seems to undervalue this magnificent structure, with the considerable tourism benefits being greatly understated. One excellent way to experience the full scale of the bridge is to take the 5-6km circular walk across it using both footways at the west and east sides of the bridge.

The combined foot and cycleways are toll free and permit you to stroll across the structure at your own speed taking in the excellent panoramic views from your elevated position, high above the Humber's muddy waters. As you walk from the anchorage towards to the tower the full scale of the

structure is awesome. Then walking onto the main centre span over the river you have a sensation of flying as you look over the handrail down to the small craft in the river below. This walk can be started from either side of the bridge, crossing under the roadway at the opposite end to return by the opposite footway.

The north bank Humber Bridge County Park is a haven for wildlife and plants, with a series of circular way marked routes that can provide interesting short rambles through the trees. Much of the park is formed around the former chalk quarries so some care should be taken to keep children away from the steep faces. Public facilities and cafes are available along with a Tourist Information centre that can inform you of other areas of interest around the County.

River traffic continues to increase with the resurgence of the ports of Hull and Goole. Also a large number of pleasure craft now use this area of the river following the multi-million pound developments of Hull's old town docks into commercial marinas. This has generated new supporting industries filling a small area vacated by the fall of the larger shipyards. Also the glamour of national power boat racing along the wide river has added to the regeneration of the water fronts.

Fact File: Humber Bridge Circular

Start/Finish: Humber Br. car parks, off Ferriby Rd., Hessle. Grid Ref: TA 021258. A flat walk over bridge footpaths (slopes or steps at start and finish).
Max. Length of Walk: 8km (5 miles). Typical Time: 2.5 hours.
OS maps: Landranger 107, Pathfinder: 696, (TA 02/12), Explorer 281 & 293.
Public Transport: Bus service over bridge.
Refreshments: Shops & cafe at bridge car parks.
Points of Special Interest: Panoramic river views from bridge. Take care in strong winds (read warning signs on bridge).
Tourist Information: Office at Humber Br. car parks. Tel: (01482) 640852.
Cycling: Complete route suitable for cycles, (ramps by-pass steps up to bridge).

Walk 4: BARTON WATERFRONT to NEW HOLLAND.

At the east side of the Humber Bridge south anchorage, a view point and car parks are again provided with public facilities. The nearby Clay Pits are now part of a small nature reserve centred around a series of ponds marking the site of the former tile and brick workings along this stretch of the Humber foreshore. A small heritage centre located here details the many former industrial workings and also informs how nature has reclaimed the flooded pits.

The foreshore at Barton Waterside is the official start of the Viking Way long distance footpath. It also provides an excellent location as the start/finish of a number of circular walks that can take you along the river bank eastward to New Holland and westwards to South Ferriby, then down onto the Lincolnshire Wolds. Although not as high as the Yorkshire Wolds they have the same idyllic quiet chalk dales peppered with small picturesque villages.

To walk the 7km from the Humber Bridge south car park to Barrow Haven and New Holland, it is necessary to follow the road inland at the side of the Haven towards the town centre. On reaching the railway station, (if one can refer to the miserable remains of the single line platform and bus shelter as a station?), cross to the east of the Haven and head back to the Humber river bank at Barton Waterside. The next 3km of walking is sandwiched between the river on your left and the flooded clay pits to your right.

On reaching Barrow Haven, you need to walk inland for 200m to cross over the tidal waters of the Haven at the side of the railway bridge and station beyond, before continuing back along the river bank the 2km to New Holland Pier. As the Humber Bridge dominates the view behind you, so the long pier stretching out into the muddy waters of the river dominates the view in front. This was the last location for the Humber Ferries crossing over the Humber to Corporation Pier on the north bank at Hull, but has found a new use as a bulk handling terminal for river traffic since the demise of the ferry paddle steamers.

Like Barrow Haven you can walk south through the village and head back to Barton, or continue another 2km east along the Humber river bank before turning inland. This latter route will add a further 4km to your ramble before you cross the railway line again and head west through New Holland

Around the Humber Bridge

Map No. 4. Barton Waterfront

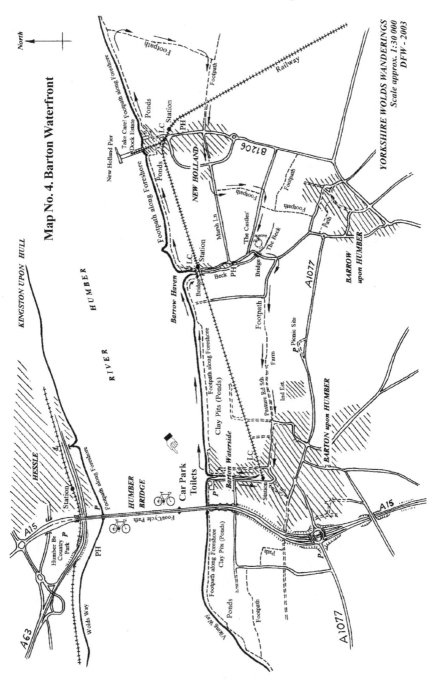

YORKSHIRE WOLDS WANDERINGS
Scale approx. 1:30 000
DFW - 2003

North

KINGSTON UPON HULL

HESSLE

R I V E R   H U M B E R

Barrow Haven

New Holland Pier

Take Care! Footpath along Foreshore
Dock Estate

Ponds

NEW HOLLAND

B1206

Station
LC
PH

Footpath

Railway

Footpath along Foreshore

Ponds

LC
Station
Beck
PH
Bridges
Bridge

Marsh Ln

The Castles'

The Beck

Bridge

Footpath

Path

BARROW
upon HUMBER

A1077

Footpath

P Picnic Site

Farm

Pasture Rd Sdn

Ind Est

BARTON upon HUMBER

Station
LC

P

Barton Waterside

Clay Pits (Ponds)

Footpath along Foreshore

HUMBER
BRIDGE

Humber Br
Country
Park P

PH

Station

Footpath along Foreshore

A15

P

Car Park
Toilets

Foot/Cycle Path

Wolds Way

A63

P

A15

Path

A1077

Viking Way

Clay Pits (Ponds)

Footpath along Foreshore

Ponds

Footpath

41

village. After 1km walking westwards along Marsh Lane, you now take the path to the left and over the field to Hann Lane where a right turn along the narrow road will bring you to 'The Castles', marked on the OS map as 'Motte and Baileys'. This group of earth mounds are believed to be of Saxon or Danish origin, and could have been a fortification or a burial ground.

After crossing The Beck (Barrow Haven) head westerly, the 3km back along the path past South Marsh Farm and along the lane called Pasture Road South into Butts Road. You are now back at Barton railway station just 1km from the Humber Bridge car park to the north. Alternatively a short walk to the south brings you to the shops and cafes that make up Barton town centre.

Fact File: Barton Waterfront to New Holland

Start/Finish: Humber Bridge south car park. Grid ref: TA 028234. A flat circular walk close to the Humber river bank.
Location: Barton clay pits at Barton Waterside, 1.5km north of town centre.
Max. length of main walk: 17km (10.5 miles), typical time around 4 to 5 hours.
Length of shorter ramble: 12km (7.5 miles), time 2.5 hours, (Barrow Haven circular).
OS maps: Landranger 112, Pathfinder 696 (TA 02/12), Explorer 281. Limited train service to Barton upon Humber, Barrow Haven and New Holland. Shops and pubs in Barton upon Humber and New Holland, pub near Barrow Haven.
Points of special interest: Humber Bridge, Barton Claypits, wildlife on ponds and river. Walkers should take special care around Barrow Haven and New Holland dock estate, these are busy industrial areas with many vehicle movements. You will have plenty of opportunities to use a pair of binoculars on the wild life and shipping along the Humber.
Cycling: All the off road sections are footpaths, so no bikes please. A short look at the OS map will reveal an array of quiet country lanes to form an enjoyable circular ride from the Humber Bridge cycle way.

Around the Humber Bridge

Walk 5: BARTON UPON HUMBER to BRIGG.

As the map indicates, a number of lengthy rambles can be taken all the way down to the old market town of Brigg, but if you only want a few hours stroll, then a number of alternative paths let you shorten the walk to suit your mood. Alternatively, a circular walk similar to the one described to New Holland can be taken to view the clay pits to the west of the Bridge car park. Walk along the river bank westwards for around 3km, then back eastward using the path that takes you past South Cliff Farm, (this provides a ninety minute walk of just over 5km in length).

Walking towards South Ferriby from Barton Waterside is also around 5km. This hour long walk by the river takes you past many of the flooded clay pits that stretch over 8km along the river bank. A good view is maintained across the Humber, from the bridge westwards. The flat 2km long Read's Island comes into view just beyond South Ferriby. This island apparently developed as the result of a ship wreck many centuries ago, with the mud and silt slowly building up around the ship's hull.

On reaching South Ferriby you have the option of continuing along the Humber bank until you reach The New River Ancholme at Ferriby Sluice, where you can turn south on this totally flat route and walk the 14km down to Brigg. A number of circular nature walks are way marked from a car park and public toilets at this location. The New River Ancholme has the appearance of a canal but is very much an important river, draining a large area of the surrounding farm land at the foot of the Wolds. The path south starts next to the swing bridge down a few steps and is squeezed between the river and a drainage dyke for a few kilometres.

Alternatively, make for the church tower at South Ferriby and take the gentle climb onto the Wolds giving you a superb view to the west. It is worth having a look at the church at South Ferriby, which has often given its parishioners problems by having an apparent wish to slide down the hill side upon which it has been constructed.

The track here is still part of the Viking Way for 2km, before turning east at Horkstow Wolds to follow the minor road for 1.5km, prior to heading south-east. This part of the route is a bridleway, (so a cycle can be used), as the walk takes you over the A15 Humber Bridge road in a deep chalk cutting below. Once over this bridge, (which carries the B1206 to New Holland), you are heading south-east at the side of the A15 dual carriageway.

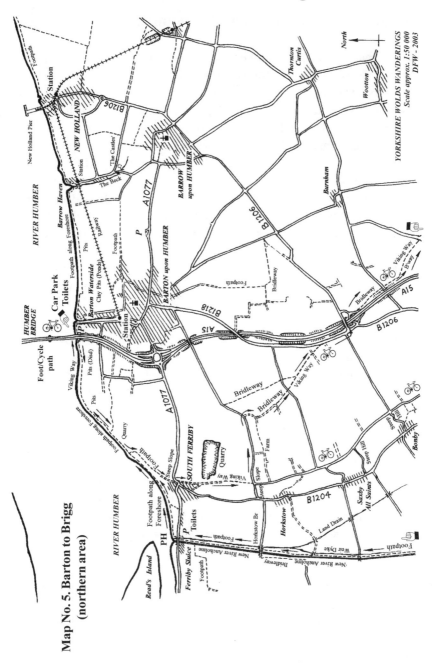

Map No. 5. Barton to Brigg (northern area)

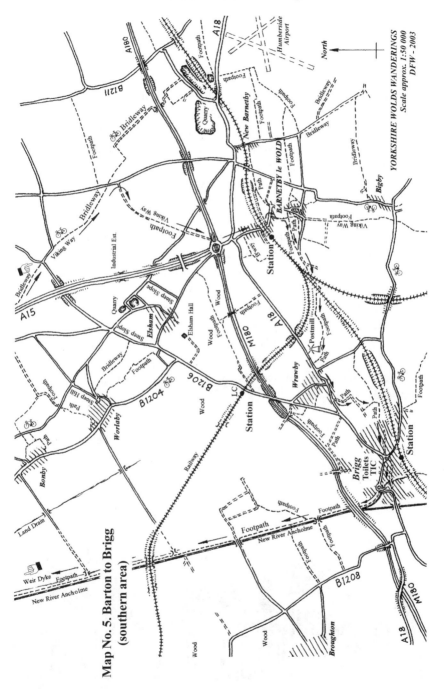

Map No. 5. Barton to Brigg (southern area)

YORKSHIRE WOLDS WANDERINGS
Scale approx. 1:50 000
DFW - 2003

The walk passes a few minor lanes before turning to the south-west, about 3km to 4km north of Barnetby le Wold and still part of the Viking Way.

The busy A15/A180 interchange is crossed along with the old A18 just to the north of the village. Barnetby le Wold stands at a still busy railway junction with railway lines converging from Scunthorpe, Gainsborough, Market Rasen and the Grimsby, Immingham area. You need to make for the south side of the village to pick up a number of footpaths that will take you meandering westerly towards Wrawby with its Postmill and then to Brigg, about 6km from Barnetby le Wold.

Make your way into the traffic free pedestrianised centre of Brigg town where public facilities and a Tourist Information Office are located. You can use the New River Ancholme route to take you back northwards for 14km in a very direct line to the Humber at Ferriby Sluice. If you are on a cycle use the A18 and B1206 north easterly for a few kilometres, to give you access back up to the Wolds and follow the minor lane that runs along the top of the escarpment above the villages of Worlaby, Bonby and Saxby All Saints.

This lane will eventually take you back to South Ferriby. Alternatively you can enter Barton upon Humber from the south side by turning east after passing near to Saxby All Saints and follow the minor roads and bridleways that take you over the A15 and down through the town and back to the waterside.

Barton Railway Station c. 1985

Around the Humber Bridge

The routes are described in very general terms. By using the maps in this book as a guide, make a detailed study of the OS map (Landranger 112, Explorer 281) and choose the length and type of rambling you prefer to gain your full enjoyment on this part of the Lincolnshire Wolds. With the opening of the Humber Bridge giving greater access to people on the north bank, many more people are learning of the tranquil delights of walking and cycling in this part of the county.

Fact File: Barton upon Humber to Brigg

Start/Finish: Humber Bridge, Barton Waterside. Grid ref: TA 028234. A full days walk over undulating Wolds, returning by a level route.

Location: Barton Waterside, 1.5km north of town centre.

Max. length of walk returning to start: 50km (31 miles), typical time a full day, 10 hours brisk walking.

Max. length of walk to Brigg: 30km (19 miles), time up to 6 hours, (one way).

Length of short ramble: (South Ferriby circular) 12km (7.5 miles), time 3 hours plus.

OS maps: Landranger 112, Pathfinder: the complete route wanders onto six different sheets, the most useful two are 707 & 719 (TA 01/11 & TA 00/10), Explorer 281.

Pubs and shops at Barton upon Humber, South Ferriby, Barnetby, Wrawby and Brigg.

Rail stations and bus service at Barton upon Humber and Brigg.

Special points of interest: Humber Bridge, Barton clay pits, Wrawby Postmill, Elsham Hall country and wildlife park.

Tourist information: Market Place, Brigg. Tel: (01652) 657053.

Cycling: Although there are no steep hills, the complete circular route would take you a full day. Plenty of options to reduce the walk, or make it one way if you can arrange transport back to your start point. For cyclists, a short ride along the roads to South Ferriby will let you have 15km on the bridleways down to the B1211 near Humberside Airport. After using roads again to reach Brigg, an enjoyable return to Barton can be made along the quiet lane running parallel to the B1204 with excellent views from your elevated location on the Lincolnshire Wolds.

Chapter 4

THE SOUTHERN YORKSHIRE WOLDS

Walk 6: BRANTINGHAM DALE CIRCULAR.

At the point where the Wolds meet the Humber, the chalk hills forming a natural obstacle, forced early transport routes to and from Hull to follow the lower land along the river bank. What is now the A63 trunk road originally ran through the villages of North Cave and South Cave but then headed south by the old Roman road to steer a route around the Wolds escarpment, then east through the villages of Elloughton, Welton, Melton, North Ferriby and Hessle before entering the town of Hull.

Not surprisingly the first railway line into the port of Hull also clung close to the river shoreline, from Leeds to Selby and Hull, opening throughout in 1840. The line was very level with only a relatively short cutting through the chalk hills at Hessle. Level tracks were a necessity for the early railways as their locomotives were not capable of pulling heavy loads up extensive gradients, or braking the train on the downward side.

As a consequence, the villages in this area became inhabited by a very early type of commuter. Rather than having to live close to their place of work in the centre of Hull and the docks; merchants, bankers and company owners could now use the train to travel into the town each day. This is the reason that many large Victorian villas were built for their wealthy occupants close to the railway stations at Hessle, Ferriby and Brough.

As industry developed with the railways in the 19th century, so this railway became the main artery to and from Hull. The port trade boomed, many new docks were built to cope with the extra trade until 10km of docks stretched from Dairycoates in the west of the city to Saltend in the east. Massive railway marshalling sidings were constructed, with the Priory sidings to the west of Hull having no fewer than seventy rails in parallel to hold the thousands of wagons.

The west Hull villages have continued to grow over the years but in a more balanced manner, with a large number of the workforce wanting to enjoy a village way of life whilst still working in the city. These villages share a pleasant array of circular footpaths that can soon have you away from the hustle and bustle of every day life.

The suggested circular routes shown on the map can be started at many locations, though I have described the walks using Brantingham as

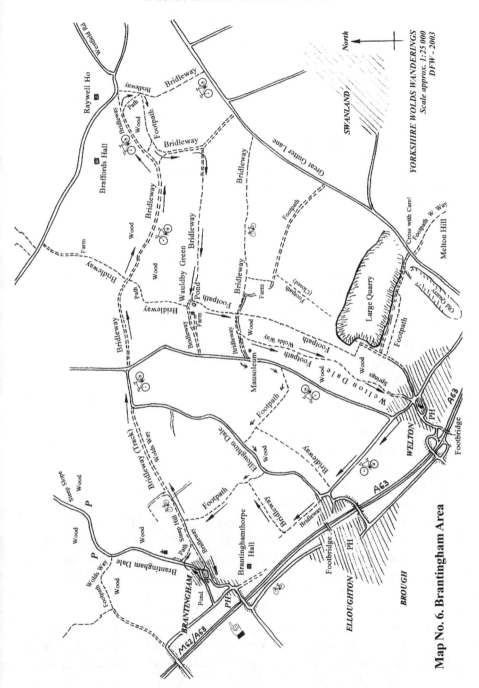

YORKSHIRE WOLDS WANDERINGS
Scale approx. 1:25 000
DFW - 2003

North

Map No. 6. Brantingham Area

the start/finish. As most of the villages have limited space for parking, be willing to be flexible if you find that a village green is already saturated with cars when you arrive. Just move on to the next village or lay-by and start your ramble from that location.

Although a small amount of building has taken place at Brantingham, it remains a very pleasant quiet village, complete with pond and a number of large houses with considerable character. Just a short distance to the south-east stands the large Elizabethan style country house at Brantinghamthorpe. This was the home of Christopher Sykes, (son of the rather eccentric Sir Tatton Sykes, 4th Baron of Sledmere House), in the 19th century. He had the house enlarged and remodelled between 1868 and 1882, and often hosted large parties for his close friend the Prince of Wales, later King Edward V11.

The lavish spreads that were expected by the royal visitor almost bankrupted Christopher Sykes. Indeed it was his financial difficulties that steered the Prince to be the house guest of the Wilsons at Tranby Croft, Anlaby, and the infamous Baccarat Scandal that rocked Victorian society in 1890.

More recently the house has changed ownership on a number of occasions, but still stands on the rising ground just to the north side of the A63 trunk road, that was built in the late 1960s to by pass the village of Elloughton.

With your transport out of the way leave the village pond area and walk north-east along Brantingham Dale towards All Saints Church, a distance of about 500m. Just before you reach the church a footpath is marked to the right heading up the steep slope of the field. As you climb the grassy slope, enjoy the view of the church and the dale beyond.

On reaching the minor road turn left and walk up the steep hill (you could have walked all the way up this lane, but you would have missed the view of the village church and Brantingham Dale). You can now follow this lane for 5km to Raywell. It is a pleasant walk, sometimes on grass, sometimes on a quiet country lane and with a succession of paths leading to the left and right (as the map shows you can use these paths to make your circular walk shorter).

Before setting off on the next leg, pause here at the top of the steep hill out of Brantingham and look back at the panorama along the Humber. On a clear day you will see across to the West Riding, notable are the numerous

All Saints Church, Brantingham Dale

power stations of the Aire valley. As you progress towards Raywell you will catch sight of Braffords Hall to the north, then Raywell House with Riplingham Road winding past.

Unless you want to walk on to Eppleworth, you change directions here and head south, then east, then south again. A path takes you past Little Wauldby Farm then onto Wauldby Manor Farm. This tranquil location is the meeting place for four public right of way by the large pond that is usually home to a numerous species of birds and other wildlife.

Your options again let you choose a number of paths southwards to Welton village, or eastward to Elloughton Dale, then on to Brantingham again to complete your circular walk. Look at the map and plan your route through the woods and down the dales. Welton, Elloughton and Brantingham all have pleasant village pubs serving food, and a few local shops are available with the ever dependable Mars Bars and drinks.

Although never far from the main east-west transport routes, these southern Yorkshire Wolds are free of traffic noise and pollution and surprisingly alive with wildlife, thus making for an exhilarating few hours of walking. If you go for the longest route you will have covered around 14km, which will probably take you four to five hours with a few stops to breath in the views.

Fact File: Brantingham Dale

Start/Finish: Brantingham village pond. Grid ref: SE 941296. A country walk with gentle slopes, a few steeper hills.
Location: To east of A63 interchange at South Cave or Welton.
Max. length of main walk: 14km (9 miles), typical time up to 4 hours.
Length of shorter ramble: 9km (5.5 miles), time 2.5 hours.
OS maps: Landranger 106, Pathfinder: 695 & 686, (SE 82/92 & SE 83/93), Explorer 293.
Limited bus service to Brantingham & Elloughton.
Pub & shop at Brantingham village.
Cycling: Good elevated views over the Humber. With a little adjustment, (to avoid footpaths only sections), much of route can be covered by cycle.

Brantingham Village Pump

Walk 7: SOUTH CAVE to DREWTON DALE.

On the route of the Roman Road, Ermine Street, South Cave village is located 4km north of Brough. Over the years the old village heart has become extended, stretching out from West End, on the road to North Cave, to Beverley Road 3km to the east. Between the two distinctive parts of the village stands Cave Castle (not a castle but a relatively new country house built around 1791) on the site of two former houses, the main one known as East Hall close to the church of All Saints. Everthorpe Hall between North and South Cave has been swallowed up by the Youth Custody Centre that has gradually expanded on that site over the past forty years. North Cave, rather smaller than South Cave still retains more of the village atmosphere, with the main street being little changed.

It was in the early 1930s that the Cave bypass was built, prior to this, all road traffic to and from Hull passed through both North Cave and South Cave on route for Booth Ferry or Selby Toll Bridge. The two villages were both served by the Hull and Barnsley Railway whose station at North Cave had the rather curious distinction of being further south than the station serving its neighbour at South Cave.

Parking is again limited in both villages so when starting your ramble please take care where your vehicle is left. As the map shows you can lengthen your circular walk to suit your preferred distance.

Starting close to All Saints Church by the entrance to Cave Castle (now a golf club and hotel), walk along the road westward and find the path heading north to Everthorpe village just over 1km away. Then take the quiet winding lane north-west to join the path heading north into North Cave by the church, also called All Saints. Here is the southern boundary to the parkland around Hotham Hall built in the 1720s. Originally this area of the parkland was part of North Cave Hall located close to the church. This was demolished in the early part of the 19th century after financial difficulties forced its sale to the owner of Hotham Hall, Mr Robert Burton. A short detour west along the road brings you to a number of small shops and a public house.

Turning east walk past the church and get back across the fields for 2km, using the path from Manor Farm to Drewton Farm. Cross the busy A1034 carefully and continue east past Drewton Manor along side the old Hull and Barnsley Railway line. You now have a number of options walking north towards the B1230 Walkington Road. All of these paths rise up through the woods to give you a splendid view south across the Humber estuary.

One path heads north just past Drewton Manor, climbing up to West Hill Farm, and on to the Walkington Road. A second branches off this path eastward past St Austin's Stone, at the head of the wooded Austin's Dale. Probably the most interesting to take however, is the third path that climbs up through Drewton Dale, past Diamond Cottage and alongside Drewton Wold until the main B1230 road is reached. Here, you only have a short distance to walk along the road-side verge before turning south and onto the paths again where you head down into Low Hunsley Plantation in East Dale. Here, for a longer walk, you can link up with walk 8 detailing rambles around Newbald.

After 2km walking down hill through the woods, the substantial railway cutting west of Sugar Loaf Tunnel is reached. Steep steps take you down to the original trackbed which is now part of the Wolds Way. You can now use the old trackbed to walk westwards to Weedley Springs. Although this is a very wide track, it is not designated a bridleway and thus is unsuitable for cycles.

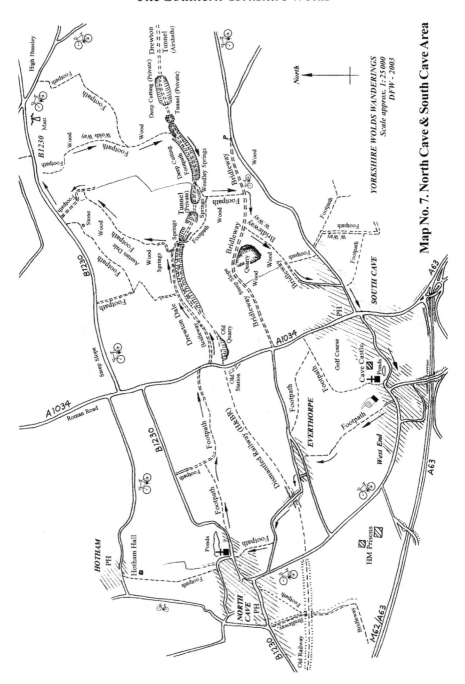

Map No. 7. North Cave & South Cave Area

YORKSHIRE WOLDS WANDERINGS
Scale approx. 1:25 000
DFW - 2003

You leave the railway trackbed by a style to your left, around 200m east of Weedley Tunnel. The path now climbs along the edge of a steep cliff down to the springs. This cliff was actually created by the railway builders in the 1880s. Unaware of the exact location of the springs, it was intended that the railway was to be built on a line further south, without the need for a short tunnel at Weedley. In view of the problems the fresh water springs created, it was decided to re-route the railway slightly further north and tunnel through the hill, thus clear of the springs. Again you have the choice whether to walk westwards back to Drewton, or turn southwards. This latter path takes you up the field towards Little Wold Plantation and the few kilometres south-west back down into South Cave.

You will notice that the Wolds Way path continues south towards Brantingham linking up with the paths in the previous walk. A short walk through South Cave village brings you back to the starting point at All Saints Church, West End.

Fact File: South Cave to Drewton Dale

Start/Finish: West End, South Cave. Grid ref: SE 915308. A walk through many southern Wolds dales. Mainly with gentle hills although a little steeper around Drewton & High Hunsley. Good views from High Hunsley, part of old Hull & Barnsley Railway, Weedley springs & woods.
Location: 2km North-west of A63/A1034 interchange, on North Cave road.
Max. length of walk: 16km (10 miles), typical time 4 hours.
Length of shorter ramble: 11km (7 miles), around 2.5 hours, (lots of options).
OS maps: Landranger 106, Pathfinder, 686, (SE 83/93), Explorer 293.
Limited bus service through North & South Cave.
Pubs & shops in both North & South Cave village centres.
Cycling: Use of minor roads can give you a pleasant 20-25km bike ride to North Cave, Hotham, South Newbald, High Hunsley, Riplingham, Low Drewton & back to South Cave.

Walk 8: NEWBALD AREA.

The two villages of North Newbald and South Newbald are located just to the east of the A1034, the line of the Roman Road from South Cave to Market Weighton. North Newbald is the larger of the two villages and has a few shops, and two public houses serving food. Just south of the village green, the large church of St Nicholas serves the two villages and has some attractive features that merit a quiet stroll around, particularly the huge tower and fine Norman doorway.

Parking on the roadside in the villages may create problems, but a little common sense will find you a suitable wide verge on one of the country lanes out of the way of large farming machinery. Three good options exist to provide you with circular walks of 7km, 12km or 18km in length, all of which can be started close to North Newbald. You can also link up with the walks to the south from the Drewton area.

Leaving North Newbald village take the lane leading to the main A1034 road to Market Weighton. Cross this road and walk due west along the bridleway following the narrow lane, then track for 2.5km, just past The Cotts. Here the bridleway is crossed by a footpath through the woods and you turn north, walking through Houghton Moor for 2km towards Castle Farm and Houghton Hall. Please note the woods are private, so keep to the path. The Georgian style Houghton Hall was built around 1765 for Mr Philip Langdale and the lake and parkland set out over the following years. It is now the home of Lord and Lady Manton.

Continuing your ramble, you turn to your right to walk the next 1km easterly into Sancton village. The church of All Saints to the north of the village is worth a look at with its unusual 15th century octagonal shaped tower with lantern styled top.

Cross the main road again near to the church and walk the 3km north-east to Arras Wold. As you gain height so the view westward becomes impressive. On a clear day a large area of flat farming land can be viewed with the ever dominant power stations on the sky line at Drax, Eggborough and Ferrybridge. On reaching the quiet lane at Arras, head south past Hessleskew Farm and keep walking due south when the lane turns right, (down to Sancton), part of the Wolds Way footpath.

At Hessleskew Gate you will observe a path from the west. A quick look at the map will confirm that this is the very pleasant, but shorter route,

Yorkshire Wolds Wanderings

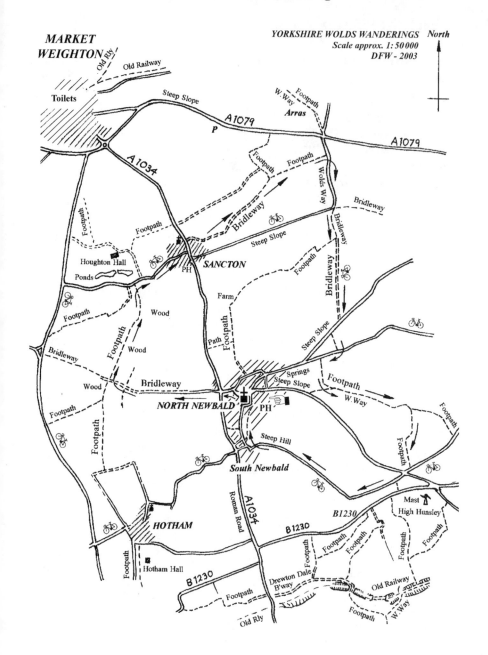

Map No. 8. Newbald Area

you could have taken from North Newbald, 4km away (a nice advantage of the shorter route is that no roads are crossed). Continue south over the brow of the hill and past the OS trig point, then the steady descent down to the lane over Newbald Wold.

If you just want a short walk, North Newbald is less than 2km west down this lane, but for a longer trek, take the path leading south again, then after another short dog-leg walk south-east along the grassy dale to Monckton Walk. This 3km in the dale is very pleasant walking, with another option to take a path back west down to Newbald.

600m before you reach Monckton Walk, you can follow the path coming down from the south. You have a steady climb out of the dale up to the quiet country lane, the unclassified road from South Newbald to Walkington. Walk along this road to the west, crossing over the busier road from Little Weighton to North Newbald

Here, you are close to High Hunsley radio mast and you will also pass the path leading southwards which follows the Wolds Way route down to Lower Hunsley Plantation and Weedley Springs. Stay on the quiet lane as it turns north-west and down the long hill into South Newbald village. It is now just under 1km north along the village lane back to the start in North Newbald and some much needed refreshments.

Fact File: Newbald Area Walks

Start/Finish: North Newbald village green. Grid ref: SE 913367. A flat start followed by gentle slopes over the Wolds.
Location: Just east of A1034, 6km north of South Cave.
Max. length of walk: 21km (13 miles), typical time: 5 hours.
Length of shorter walk: 9km (5.5 miles), time: 2 hours.
OS maps: Landranger: 106. Pathfinder: 686 & 675, (SE 83/93), Explorer 291 & 293. Pubs & shops in North Newbald village centre. Limited bus service to village.
Cycling: Interesting churches at North Newbald & Sancton, Houghton Hall, (not open to public), views from Arras Wold. Use minor roads & bridleways to form 25km cycle route; North Newbald to Hotham, Sancton, and Walkington, return via High Hunsley and South Newbald back to start.

Walk 9: SKIDBY to WALKINGTON CIRCULAR.

Just to the west of the A164 trunk road, the village of Skidby has the distinction of a wide choice of paths converging from all directions. Skidby is best known throughout the area for its Windmill and the Half Moon public house serving monster size Yorkshire Puddings!

The windmill at Skidby is of particular interest, not just because it is in full working order, but because it never really fell out of use. Built in 1821 by the local Thompson family, it was further extended in the middle of the 19th century with the various storage building constructed around the base. This necessitated the raising of the mill to its present height so that the sails cleared the roof tops of the new storage area. Amazingly the mill was still in commercial use in the 1950s, by which time its unique status was beginning to be appreciated as many of the county's other mills were now long disused.

As a working mill it was offered to the local authority and the Council have since managed the building, steadily undertaking a number of major repairs (ably assisted by a local army of volunteers, keen to see the mill wheels turning on a regular bases). It is generally accepted as being the finest example of a working tower windmill in the east of England and now includes a farming museum and craft centre, so it is well worth a visit and flour actually ground at the mill can be purchased by the public.

A close inspection of the internal workings of the windmill may greet you with a degree of surprise when you see just how complex the gearing mechanism is for controlling the speed of the sails.

Paths and bridleways can take you north and east from Skidby to Risby, Walkington and Beverley. Southwards around the windmill and to Eppleworth, or west to Rowley, Wauldby and Raywell.

A pleasant few hours stroll is to leave the church of Saint Michael in the centre of the village and walk due north to Risby and Bentley. A bridleway commences along Church Lane opposite the church and next to the village hall. After crossing an undulating field, it leads you through a short wood. The ground is now rising slowly to take you along to the narrow track towards Risby (a large farm house to the north west). Continue over the lane at the side of Fishpond Wood and another 1km to the Bentley corners. Since the opening of Beverley bypass, this road has seen a pleasing drop in the amount of road traffic, but if you walk along it to reach Walkington, keep well into the side for safety.

Skidby Windmill

Yorkshire Wolds Wanderings

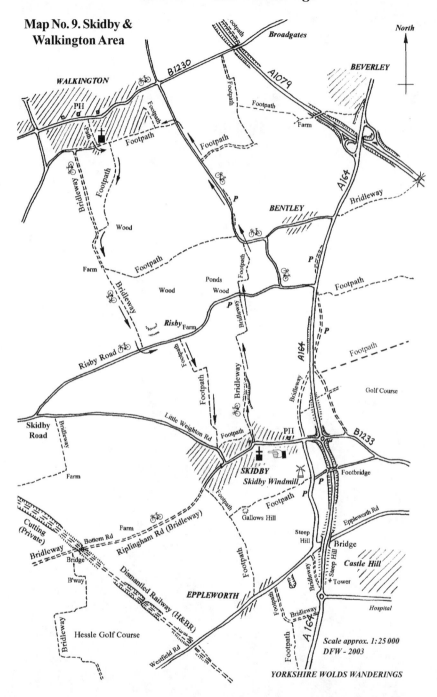

**Map No. 9. Skidby &
Walkington Area**

North

Footpath

Broadgates

BEVERLEY

WALKINGTON

B1230

A1079

PH

Footpath

Footpath

Footpath

Farm

Footpath

A164

Path

Footpath

Bridleway

Footpath

Bridleway

Footpath

P

BENTLEY

Bridleway

Farm

Wood

Footpath

P

Bridleway

Wood

Ponds

Wood

Footpath

P

Risby Farm

Bridleway

P

Bridleway

Risby Road

Footpath

Bridleway

A164

Golf Course

Footpath

Skidby
Road

Bridleway

Little Weighton Rd

Footpath

Bridleway

PH

B1233

Farm

Footpath

SKIDBY

Skidby Windmill

Footbridge

Cutting
(Private)

Farm

Footpath

Gallows Hill

Footpath

P

Bridleway

Bottom Rd

Riplingham Rd (Bridleway)

Steep
Hill

Eppleworth Rd

Bridge

Bridge

Steep Hill

Castle Hill

B'way

Dismantled Railway (H&BR)

EPPLEWORTH

Bridleway

Tower

Hospital

Bridleway

Hessle Golf Course

Footpath

Bridleway

A164

Westfield Rd

Footpath

**Scale approx. 1:25 000
DFW - 2003**

YORKSHIRE WOLDS WANDERINGS

The Southern Yorkshire Wolds

The small hamlet of Bentley can be seen to the east (with a path crossing the busy A164 to continue to the south side of Beverley). Walking just a short distance north along the road, a path leads west to Risby Park, or continuing along the road, a further path leads east to Beverley via the Westwood. Another few hundred metres further, and another path takes you due west, to the south side of Walkington village (by the playing field). Look at the map to check that you use the correct footpath.

The circular route back to Skidby and Halfpenny Gate, heads off to the south of Walkington, but it is worth walking a few extra paces west to look at All Hallows Church, standing majestically in the trees. A short snicket also leads to the village centre and the three welcoming pubs.

The return walk southwards through the parkland tells you that this was once part of a country estate with long established trees to both sides of the path. Walk past Halfpenny Gate cottages and Risby Park Farm as you continue to travel south back to the narrow lane to Risby. Walk east for a short distance until a sign directs you south again to Skidby. At this point look back to the site of the former country mansion at Risby. You will soon detect the area where Risby Hall once stood with the terraced gardens to the south.

This fine house built in the 1680s was demolished after two major fires in the 1770s and 1780s. It is just over 1km back over the fields to Skidby village for the challenge of a giant Yorkshire pudding with gravy and a glass or two of beer.

Fact File: Skidby to Walkington Circular

Start/Finish: St. Michael's Church, Skidby village green. Grid ref: TA 105337. A circular walk over undulating fields.
Location: Skidby village centre, 1km west of A164 roundabout.
Max. length of walk: 9km (5.5 miles), typical time: 2.5 hours.
Length of shorter walk: 6km (4 miles), time under 2 hours.
OS maps: Landranger 106, Pathfinder: 687 & 686, (TA 03/13). Explorer 293. Limited bus service through Skidby to Little Weighton & Walkington. Pubs & shops in villages enroute.
Points of special interest: Skidby Windmill & Museum, site of Risby House.
Cycling: With adjustments at Bentley & Little Weighton, the route is suitable for bikes giving a circular ride of around 15km.

Walk 10: SKIDBY to WAULDBY GREEN and EPPLEWORTH.

The route west out of Skidby along Riplingham road can be used for a short circular walk that takes you around to the windmill site by Gallows Hill. This clump of trees on a slightly raised mound was reputedly the site of the local gallows, although most parishes had such a facility, few records exists to confirm the origins of the site. A slightly longer circular route takes you down to the hamlet of Eppleworth, and the walk back up Skidby Hill joining the shorter route at Skidby Windmill. Riplingham Road (also known as Bottom Road) can also be used for longer walks to Rowley, 4km from Skidby, or, south-west down to Wauldby and taking the route back to Raywell.

About 2km along Riplingham Road the track passes under an old railway bridge, once the property of the Hull, Barnsley and West Riding Junction Railway and Dock Company Limited. This railway was one of the last main line routes to be constructed in England from 1880 to its opening in 1885. The independent railway and dock was built at a tremendous cost by the frustrated businessmen of Hull, with the full backing of the Town Corporation, in an effort to break the transport monopoly then held by the North Eastern Railway Company.

With the North Eastern routes following the low ground along the Humber and the only other natural gap in the Wolds at Market Weighton, the Hull and Barnsley route was forced to climb over and through the difficult chalk hills between South Cave and Willerby. The result was mile after mile of very deep cuttings and three tunnels; Weedley, Sugar Loaf and the 1,933m long one at Drewton, also known as Riplingham Tunnel. In addition, the steep gradients meant higher running costs as heavy coal trains often had to be double-headed by two locomotives to pull them up the inclines.

The line had an independent existence of just under 40 years before the NER swallowed it up prior to the grouping of the railways in 1922. After the Second World War it became a target for early closure as most of the traffic could be taken on the old Hull and Selby route to reach the docks in Hull. Services were steadily cut back until the line finally closed from Little Weighton westwards in 1958, then completely in the early 1960s. Only the high level lines remain around Hull, crossing above all the main roads to reach King George Dock and Saltend.

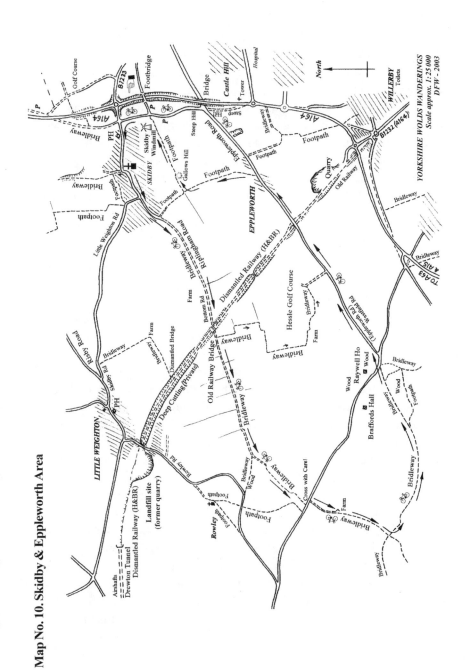

Map No. 10. Skidby & Eppleworth Area

Yorkshire Wolds Wanderings

What a great pity that we did not possess any far sighted councillors that were capable of seeing the golden benefit that this high level railway line could have brought to the Willerby and Anlaby areas, shuttling passengers by modern train to and from the City Centre each day, instead of clogging up all the inadequate artery roads with innumerable cars.

Over the years many of the Hull and Barnsley Railway landmarks have been demolished, though between Eppleworth and North Cave plenty of clues still identify the engineering feat of building this railway. As covered in walk No.7 part of the Wolds Way footpath has been routed along the old trackbed between Weedley Tunnel and Sugar Loaf Tunnel, west of Drewton Tunnel. The substantial chalk cuttings up to 30m deep still exist around the Little Weighton area and around Drewton, though each year sees more back-filling with industrial waste. The latest edition of the OS map has significantly reduced the amount of 'Dismantled Railway' shown. Sadly this costly project of the 1880s is quickly slipping into history with only old photographs left to identify this bygone age of transport.

The walk on the bridleway along Riplingham Road is easy to follow. It is in fact a full highway from the village of Skidby to just beyond the old railway bridge. This is possibly due to the original intention of the Hull and Barnsley Railway to build a station to serve the village. The first 2km are on a metalled (tarred), surface up to the railway bridge. Just after the bridge a further bridleway heads south, leading around the Hessle Golf Club to Eppleworth Road. Hessle Golf Club course was originally located on the north approach to the Humber Bridge at Hessle, but had to move in the late 1970s as building work on the Bridge enveloped the site.

To continue your walk westwards towards Rowley, the track continues for another 2km where a further bridleway branches off to the south, this time making for Wauldby Manor Farm then on to Welton Dale. By taking this path you can enjoy a circular route back towards Skidby via York Grounds Farm and Wauldby Manor Farm, then back via Braffords Hall and Raywell House onto Eppleworth Road. After 1km on Eppleworth Road you pass the south end of the bridleway around Hessle Golf Course taking you back to Skidby. Alternatively you can continue another 1.5km to the hamlet of Eppleworth, passing the site of the former five arches railway viaduct, and then north on the footpath over the fields to Skidby.

Most of these rambles are on very pleasant country tracks and if you are on a cycle please remember that the Skidby to Eppleworth route is only a footpath, so use one of the other routes to complete your circular ride. Skidby is also close to the midway point of the 'Beverley Twenty' walk from the centre of Beverley to the Humber Bridge. This walk on well marked paths is 20 miles (32km) and an excellent way to see the Southern Wolds.

Fact File: Skidby to Wauldby Green and Eppleworth

Start/Finish: Skidby Windmill car park. Grid ref: TA 022333. A circular walk with gentle hills & few road crossings.

Location: Lay-by off the old road just west of new A164 roundabout, sign posted 'Skidby Mill'.

Max. length of walk: 13km (8 miles), typical time: 3 hours.

Length of shorter ramble: 9km (5.5 miles), time 2 hours, (many options).

OS maps: Landranger 106, Pathfinder: 686 & 687, (SE 83/93 & TA 03/13) Explorer 293. Limited bus service through Skidby village. Pub & shops in village centre.

Points of special interest: Skidby Windmill & museum.

Cycling: All the route can be covered by bike except for the path from Eppleworth to Skidby Mill (use the road up Skidby hill).

Cherry Burton Village Pump

Chapter 5

BEVERLEY AND THE HUDSON WAY

Walk 11. WALKINGTON to BEVERLEY

Four kilometres to the north of Skidby is the larger village of Walkington. Well known for its three pleasant public houses, village pond and attractive main street, it is located 4km south-west of Beverley on the B1230. The 'Beverley Twenty' footpath has two options to the northern section of the route, one of them passing to the south of the village.

This path can be picked up by the church of All Hallows at the south side of the village and walked eastward towards the road, then south for 400m. At Bentley Park Farm follow the track eastward towards Butt Farm, then north to Broadgate Farm. After crossing the B1230 and the bridge over the A1079 Beverley Bypass, you turn to your left, following along the side of the bypass for almost 1km before turning east towards The Westwood and Beverley. Cross over to the north-east corner of the Westwood and York Road. You can now enter Beverley town through the North Bar, a fortified gate built almost 600 years ago.

Beverley Westwood is a large area of open common land providing an excellent playground for children, dog walkers or just simply a relaxing way to sit in the car and enjoy the wildlife and countryside. Throughout the summer months cattle graze on the pasture and horses are regularly exercised over the undulating land. Although crossed by four roads, the size of the Westwood means that you can wander well clear of road traffic, with plenty of safe areas for children to play.

The more wooded north-east corner of the Westwood is a haven for wildlife and is known locally as Burton Bushes. Without a dog at your side, you are sure to spy an abundance of animals scurrying about their business amongst the mature trees and undergrowth. The sites of two windmills can be easily seen on the Westwood: Black Mill standing high in a dominant location on the middle of the area and the now smaller former whiting mill incorporated into the Beverley Golf Course club-house to the south. The remains of a third windmill also existed along the south side of the Westwood, though little trace can be seen from of the nearby road as it is incorporated into the site of a house. It is believed that two further windmills were also located on the Westwood, though no trace of them remains today.

Beverley and the Hudson Way

Map No. 11. Walkington to Beverley

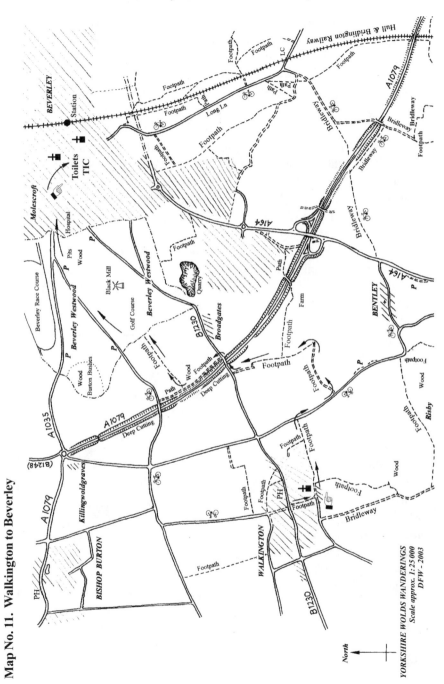

YORKSHIRE WOLDS WANDERINGS
Scale approx. 1:25 000
DFW - 2003

North

Yorkshire Wolds Wanderings

Along the northern boundary of the Westwood is the Beverley Race Course which still has a healthy diary of meetings each year on its clockwise circuit. The eastern edge of the Westwood has a fine display of large Victorian villas and the Westwood Hospital site.

The market town of Beverley has always been the administrative centre of the East Riding of Yorkshire. The central town area is little changed over the past century with the fine market area surrounded by listed buildings. Beverley Bar is the original gate into the town from the north, built in its present form in 1410. Unlike the other gates it has survived the centuries to remain a unique feature which is well worth a close inspection.

Just to the south along North Bar Within is the beautiful church of Saint Mary. Built around the 13th century on the site of an earlier Norman church and with the tower dating from the 1520s following the collapse of the previous structure. Although not as large as the famous Minster to the south of the town, this church is a real jewel and a must to have a look around. It is also famed with the credit for inspiring Lewis Carrol to create his famous novel, 'Alice Through The Looking Glass'. Walk around the inside of the church and see if you can spot the rabbit engraved into the stonework. One really wonders if the creative sculptor was perhaps, playing the fool when he created this unusual carving.

Walking south from St Mary's church and through Saturday Market, you pass the recently refurbished band stand in the cobbled area of the market place. Continuing southwards you are drawn to the magnificence of Beverley Minster dominating the skyline for miles around. This vast church was constructed over many years with most of the current structure created in the

Beverley Bar c.1900

13th and 14th centuries. Along with St Mary's, it is an indication of the wealth that must have existed in the town so many centuries ago to produce these two fine places of worship.

The many carvings that adorn both the inside and the outside of the Minster have proved a valuable record of many aspects of musical life so many years ago. Do spend some time walking around the Minster reflecting on the millions of hours of craftsmen's work that has produced this monument to Christ.

The town of Beverley has an array of traditional pubs, many shops and cafes. Public facilities are well signposted. Make good use of the Tourist Information office which is located on Butcher Row and is open all the year. Here you can learn of other attractions in and around the town, including the very interesting Museum of Army Transport just over the railway crossing on Flemingate.

Beverley is quite well served with bus and train links to the surrounding area, enabling you to tackle the 'Beverley Twenty' walk to Hessle using the train to transport you back to your starting point.

Fact File: Walkington to Beverley

Start/Finish: All Hallows Church, Walkington to Beverley Minster. Grid refs: SE 998368 & TA 038392. Generally flat walking to Beverley.

Locations: South side of Walkington, 400m from B1230 & south side of Beverley town centre.

Max. length of walk: 7km (4.5 miles) one way, time: 2 hours.

OS Maps: Landranger 106 & 107, Pathfinder: 687, (TA 03/13), Explorer 293. Bus service between Walkington & Beverley. Good array of shops & pubs in Beverley town & Walkington village centre.

Points of special interest: Beverley Westwood, Beverley Bar, St Mary's & The Minster. Museum of Army Transport currently located in Beverley. Tourist information office 34 Butcher Row, Beverley. Tel: (01482) 391672.

Cycling: By riding down to Bentley village, a cycle route can be taken into Beverley from the south side via Long Lane.

Beverley Minster

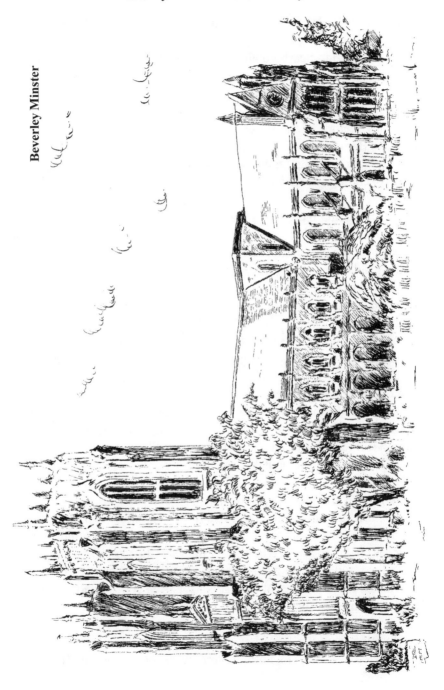

Walk 12. THE HUDSON WAY to MARKET WEIGHTON.

On the Hull to Scarborough railway line, Beverley was once also the junction for the Hull to York line which branched off the Scarborough line just to the north of the town and headed west to Market Weighton. Although this railway was quite well patronised, the line became one of the many victims of the Beeching closures in the early 1960s. Like the Hull and Barnsley line it was a double track route. It passed to the north of Cherry Burton village, then to the south of Dalton Hall and through a series of cuttings westwards until eventually arriving at Market Weighton Station.

At this station there was a major junction with the Selby to Driffield line. Whilst open, this other line, gave a direct route for West Riding traffic heading for the east coast at Bridlington, Scarborough and in later years Butlin's Holiday Camp at Filey. From Market Weighton the York line headed north-west to Pocklington, then onto Stamford Bridge and over the River Derwent on a grandiose viaduct before finally sweeping around into York from the north side.

Although it is sad to see all the waste of a derelict railway, the section of trackbed from Market Weighton through to the north of Beverley was purchased by the council and converted into a bridleway some years ago. It makes an excellent level route crossing only a few roads along its length of 16km. Depending on your view of railway history, this established walk has been named, rightly or wrongly, 'The Hudson Way,' after the 'Railway King' George Hudson. This man was responsible for promoting many of the railway lines throughout the Yorkshire area in the mid 19th century, but fell from grace after a series of financial scandals exposed his dubious dealings with promoters investments.

You can start this walk (and cycle ride) from either end, or at any of the access points along the route. Once on the line of the old railway, which is classified as a 'Permissive Bridleway' the route is easy to follow and where bridges have been removed, gentle slopes or steps have been provided. Also a number of car parks have been constructed, the largest being at Kiplingcoates former railway station where refreshments can also be purchased.

Starting from the Beverley end of the walk, a footbridge has been constructed over the new north eastern by-pass of Beverley. Also at this location a picnic area and car park are sign posted from the north side of the new road.

The route takes you north-west under the A164 to the south of Leconfield. The large former RAF base to the east of the village is now the headquarters of the Army driver training unit, with thousands of military drivers from all the forces being trained here each year. The RAF Air Sea Rescue still operates from the base with its Sea King helicopters, a common sight over East Yorkshire. To the west side of the A164 is the site of Leconfield Castle which was owned by the Percy family (along with Wressle Castle by the River Derwent, part of which is still standing). Short footpaths lead you north just off the Hudson Way to the castle site.

The walk then takes you through Cherry Burton station site, to the north side of the village and over the B1248. With the removal of the bridge thirty years ago, this is the only busy road that you need to cross at the same level. Long ramps and safety rails enable cycles and push chairs to gain access from the embankments to the road level on both sides. A further 1km west you pass under the road to Etton village (just over 500m to the north, the village also has a splendid public house selling good food). It is now 6km of very pleasant walking to Kiplingcoates Station. The old line then runs parallel to a minor road, passing a nature reserve in the old quarries, on the final 5km stretch down to Market Weighton.

Much of the route is a haven for wildlife. Of particular interest is the nature reserve in the old chalk quarries some 2km west of Kiplingcoates Station (please do not take your dog into this area and keep only to the marked paths). Throughout the existence of this railway line one peculiarity was that trains never ran on a Sunday. This was by strict order of Lord Hotham as the railway was routed through his land. This is also the reason why such a large station was built in open countryside at Kiplingcoates serving his lordship's requirements at Dalton Hall. The Hall is located a few kilometres to the north-east by the estate village of South Dalton. Built in the 1770s it is the home of the Hotham family, who also had the beautiful church of St Mary erected around 1860 with its elegant steeple over 60m high. A few kilometres east of Market Weighton, the Wolds Way footpath joins the Hudson Way from the south to share the bridleway into the town.

Public toilets are located in Market Weighton along with shops and public houses for refreshments. Two alternative routes here take the Wolds

Map No. 12. The Hudson Way (east side)

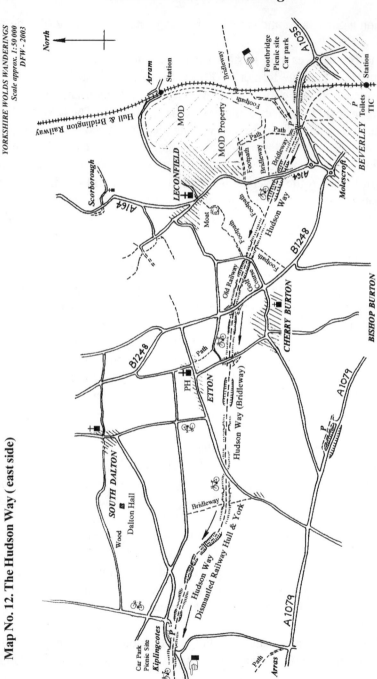

YORKSHIRE WOLDS WANDERINGS
Scale approx. 1:50 000
DFW - 2003

North

Hull & Bridlington Railway

Arram Station

Footbridge
Picnic site
Car park

A1035

Station

MOD

MOD Property

Bridleway

Footpath

Footpath

Path
Path

BEVERLEY

P
Toilets
TIC

Scorborough

A164

LECONFIELD

Moat

Footpath

Footpath

Footpath

Footpath

Bridleway

Bridleway

Hudson Way

A164

Molescroft

B1248

Old Railway

Golf Course

CHERRY BURTON

BISHOP BURTON

B1248

Path

ETTON

PH

Hudson Way (Bridleway)

A1079

P

SOUTH DALTON

Dalton Hall

Wood

Bridleway

Hudson Way

Hudson Way

Dismantled Railway Hull & York

Car Park
Picnic Site
Kiplingcotes

Path

Arras

A1079

76

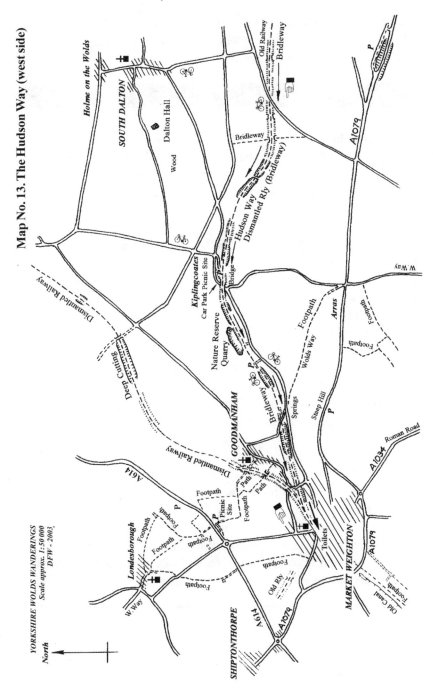

Map No. 13. The Hudson Way (west side)

YORKSHIRE WOLDS WANDERINGS
Scale approx. 1:50 000
DFW - 2003.

North

Holme on the Wolds

SOUTH DALTON

Dalton Hall

Wood

Old Railway

Bridleway

A1079

Bridleway

Hudson Way
Dismantled Rly (Bridleway)

Dismantled Railway

Bridge

Kiplingcoates
Car Park Picnic Site

Nature Reserve
Quarry

Deep Cutting

W.Way

Footpath

Footpath

Footpath

Arras

Wolds Way

Bridleway

Springs

Steep Hill

P

GOODMANHAM

Dismantled Railway

Roman Road

A1034

Footpath

P

Path

Footpath

Path

A614

Londesborough

Picnic
Site

Footpath

Footpath

Footpath

Footpath

Footpath

Toilets

MARKET WEIGHTON

A1079

W. Way

SHIPTONTHORPE

A614

A1079

Old Rly

Footpath

Old Canal

Footpath

Way footpath northwards to the small estate village of Londesborough. These routes can be used as a pleasant short circular walk of around 7km from Market Weighton to Londesborough and back.

Fact File: Hudson Way

Start/Finish: Picnic site off Beverley north eastern bypass to centre of Market Weighton. Grid refs: TA 028414 & SE 877418. A level walk along the old Hull to York railway line.

Location: North eastern bypass of Beverley 1.5km north of the Market Place to the town centre of Market Weighton on old A1079.

Max. length of walk: 16km (10 miles), typical time 4 hours, (one way).

Length of shorter walk: 10km (6.5 miles) to Kiplingcoates, 2.5 hours one way.

OS maps: Landranger 106, Pathfinder 675 & 676 (SE 84/94 & TA 04/14) Explorer 293 & 294.

Bus service between Beverley and Market Weighton. Pubs and shops at Beverley & Market Weighton town centres, cafe at Kiplingcoates station and pubs at Etton and Cherry Burton villages (1km from the rail trail route).

Points of special interest: Nature reserve in Kiplingcoates old quarry, 1.5km west of old station. Plenty of wildlife and flowers throughout route. Tourist information office 34 Butcher Row, Beverley. Tel: (01482) 391672.

Cycling: The complete route is classified as a 'Permissive Bridleway', as such you can cycle along the complete length of the track bed. By use of minor roads a pleasant circular route will bring you back to your starting point, making a round cycle ride of about 35km. Cyclists should take care passing pedestrians on the old railway as they may not hear you approaching.

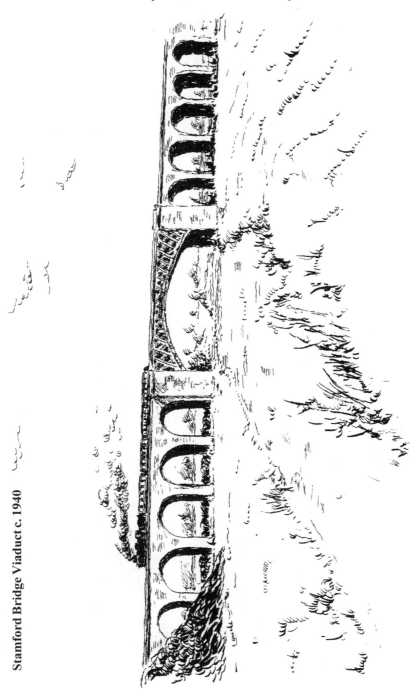

Stamford Bridge Viaduct c. 1940

Chapter 6

THE HEART OF THE WOLDS

Walk 13: MILLINGTON PASTURE and GIVENDALE.

Market Weighton is at a key location on The Wolds as the hills form a natural gap at this location. Not surprisingly advantage has been made of this slightly lower ground for the original road from the Hull and Beverley areas to York and beyond. The railway builders also saw the same importance of this area and in very speculative style George Hudson purchased the vast Londesborough Estate to the north of Market Weighton for the enormous sum of around half a million pounds in 1845. He did this not so much to secure a route for the as yet unbuilt Beverley, Market Weighton to York railway line, but to stop any other rival railway company putting a line through the Wolds in that area and gaining access to the port of Hull.

In the 17th and 18th centuries Londesborough was one of Yorkshire's major country houses set in an estate of thousands of acres covering the Wolds to the north of Market Weighton. The house was in the ownership of the Earl of Burlington who had it enlarged around 1680. A massive programme over many years saw the vast estate of 12,000 acres develop around the house with many avenues of tree lined roads converging on the mansion. Although owning many estates in England and Ireland, the successive Earls of Burlington usually spent some time at Londesborough each year.

After the death of the third Earl in 1753 the house was inherited by William Cavendish, who became the 4th Duke of Devonshire in 1755. Their family rarely visited the estate and it fell into decline. Although this great parkland still has many clues to its former glory, the house was demolished around 1819.

From old drawings and maps of the area, it is difficult to understand how such a great house could slide into history almost two centuries ago. The house was located just to the east of All Saints Church in the village where the Burlington family is commemorated.

Just a few kilometres northwards from Londesborough is the village of Nunburnholme on the edge of the Warter Priory Estate. Like its southern neighbour, Warter Priory was also one of the largest country houses in East Yorkshire.

The Heart of The Wolds

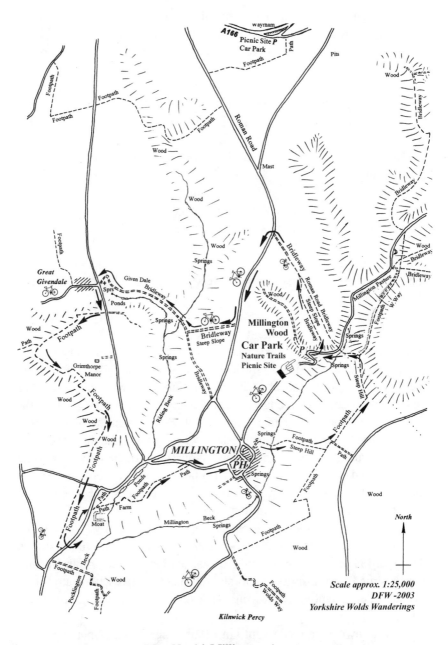

Map No. 14. Millington Area

Although starting as a modest dwelling on the site of an Augustinian priory founded in 1132, the house was enlarged in the 18th century before being purchased by Charles Henry Wilson, brother of Arthur Wilson, in the year of 1875.

With their vast family wealth created from the Wilson Line shipping fleet (the largest in the country at that time), he again set out to enlarge the house in the 1870s and 1880s until it finished up with no less than eighty bedrooms.

Sadly this house too did not survive and it is often said by local historians that of all the lost houses in the county, the demolition of Warter Priory in 1972 was an act of outrageous vandalism! There is no doubt that in its heyday, supported by incredible family wealth, Warter Priory was a palace. Room after room was extravagantly furnished, a marble stairway adorned the hall, 300 acres of formal gardens and a lake surrounded the house. This naturally required a large army of hard working and totally loyal gardeners, cooks, maids, butlers, and servants of every description to keep the house in order.

With few opportunities to better themselves in the countryside, the local people often had to be content to work on the land or in service on a nearby estate. Normally they would live in tied cottages, very often a complete village, working for the local Lord of the Manor. Well away from the effects of the industrial revolution hitting the towns and cities, this culture continued unchallenged and unchanged until the early years of the 20th century. Then with so many men called away to fight for their country, the needs of these large country estates began to feel the pressure.

In particular, with fewer people available for work, better wages could be demanded and steadily the cost of running these vast country houses increased. Many sons did not return from the trenches in France to run their father's estates compounding the problems.

Warter Priory was a huge Victorian mansion, the family shipping line drifted from the Wilson's after the deaths of Charles in 1907 and then Arthur in 1910 and the fortunes of the estate darkened. The former glorious house turned into a monster and slowly disintegrated with many of its treasures being removed following the death of Charles' wife, Florence in 1932.

Various owners moved in until in 1960s, when in the ownership of the Guinness Family Trust, the owners said that they were unable to find a

Warter Priory c. 1890

practical use for the building and in 1972 Warter Priory was razed to the ground. The rubble was unceremoniously dumped into the lake and another chapter closed on the fine country houses of Yorkshire.

In the 1990s even the church of St James in the village of Warter stood redundant, complete with a large placard outside, not calling upon you to 'Praise the Lord!' but telling you that the building was; 'For Sale.' At the north side of the churchyard is the tomb for Lord Nunburnholme. After 30 years in Parliament as Liberal MP for Hull, Charles Wilson was made a Peer one year before his death. Even the grave looks in a very sorry state amongst the weeds around the church. Though the house is now gone, the splendid scenery of the area remains for all to enjoy along the routes of various rambles.

With so many circular walks to choose from in the area around Millington Pasture, you should have a long look at the maps before you start your ramble. A car park and picnic area is located at the nature reserve by Millington Wood and a second site further north, just off the A166 at Wayrham, (4km west of Fridaythorpe). Also if you position your transport sensibly, there are other areas throughout Millington Dale and along to Huggate where you could park, but please do not expect to leave your car in a pub car park all day when you are not a paying customer!

Leaving the car park at Millington Wood, walk back onto the narrow lane winding up Millington Dale and turn immediately left, (north east). Look for the footpath sign sending you up the steep hillside. You will soon be walking almost due north towards Millington Heights. You have now joined part of the Roman Road coming up from the south, passing through the village of Warter. Various evidence of a Roman settlement has been found in this area. The path has gained height to 218 metres where it joins a narrow country lane 2km from Millington Dale. Turn sharp left (south west) along this road for just over 1km then get back onto the fields turning right (due east). You are now following a bridleway down hill towards Great Givendale. Another bridleway, (which forms part of the Minster Way), joins from the south. Continue to the north east down the steep slope and over the bridge across Whitedale Beck.

As you near the small hamlet of Great Givendale a number of springs and ponds are visible on your left, to the south of the tiny but pretty church. There is evidence of Saxon settlers around this area who dug out the clay covered chalk to form fish ponds, (but please note these ponds are located on private land, the path keeping to the north side).

After seeing the church, walk south along the lane for just a few hundred metres before taking the path to your right (west). If you are cycling, stay on the lane, as the next section is along a footpath, not a bridleway.

The path soon heads west along side Brimlands Wood for a few hundred metres, then south west steadily loosing height. Another path forks to your right, but stay on this path turning to the south east and along the top of the escarpment. After a short distance you walk around three sides of a square then along the side of Grimthorpe Wood and almost due south as the trees are left behind and the ground levels off. A minor road is crossed at right angles and after another kilometre a sharp turn to the left brings you back onto a narrow lane linking the town of Pocklington to Millington

Walk north east along the lane for around 600 metres before taking the path to your right. Crossing over the Ridings Beck you soon pass to the north side of Mill Farm and continue a very gentle rise to rejoin the lane a kilometre further along and only 500 metres from Millington Village.

Fact File: Millington Area

Start/Finish: Millington Wood car park & picnic site. Grid ref. SE 838530. A very pleasant walk with several steep slopes around Millington village.

Location: 5km north east from Pocklington town centre, on road to Huggate

Max. length of main walk. 14km (9 miles) typical time: around 4 hours plus.

Length of shorter ramble: 8km (5 miles), time: 2 hours.

OS maps: Landranger 106, Pathfinder 666 (SE 85195), Explorer 294. Pub & cafe in Millington village.

Points of special interest: Millington Woods, many nature trails through this Site of Special Scientific Interest, (SSSI). Ideal for introducing young children to the delights of nature studies.

Cycling: Once again with a little adjustment to the route a good circular cycle ride can be enjoyed using bridleways and minor roads. Some of the steeper hills on this walk make the wearing of strong shoes or boots more significant.

Millington caters for the outdoor fraternity with a welcoming public house and tea rooms in the village. The church at the north side is pleasing to view before heading for the path again to the west of the village. A steep climb ensures to reach Warren Farm and a walk along the top of the escarpment before turning to the north west along the line of the Roman Road again. After savouring the view descend down to the dale again and back to your transport in the car park picnic area of Millington Wood.

You will view the many fresh water springs in this area, no doubt an attraction to early settlers The woods are an excellent location to introduce young children to the joys of nature, with many walks marked out amongst the trees. A short look at the map will indicate the many options for varying the route of your walk or with a little adjustment making a good cycle route using the quiet lanes and bridleways.

Walk 14: WAYRHAM to FRIDAYTHORPE and HUGGATE.

A longer ramble in this area is based at the Wayrham picnic lay-by, just off the busy A166 York to Bridlington road. It is located between the summit of Garrowby Hill to the west, and Fridaythorpe village 5km to the east. Another road leads up from Huggate and North Dalton to the south-east.

To start this walk you need to leave the picnic lay-by and cross the busy A166. A footpath leads north-east down into the dale to the side of Wayrham Farm. This very pleasant path is followed for almost 3km, with a path joining from the east, then a bridleway from the west.

Here make a fairly steep climb up to Gill's Farm on the Wolds Way path. Then walking due east down to Ings Plantation in Brubber Dale, make another steep climb to reach the village of Fridaythorpe high on the wind-swept hills of the Wolds. There is a public house here and a small shop for refreshment stops. Also of interest here is the quaint village church of St. Mary. It displays many signs of the struggles that small communities have keeping such buildings in good repair against bitter winter weather in these exposed locations. The Norman tower houses a highly decorative clock of large proportions that was added to the building during restoration at the beginning of the 20th century.

From Fridaythorpe you need to cross the main A166 road again and head south. After 500m a bridleway veers off to the south-east down to

The Heart of The Wolds

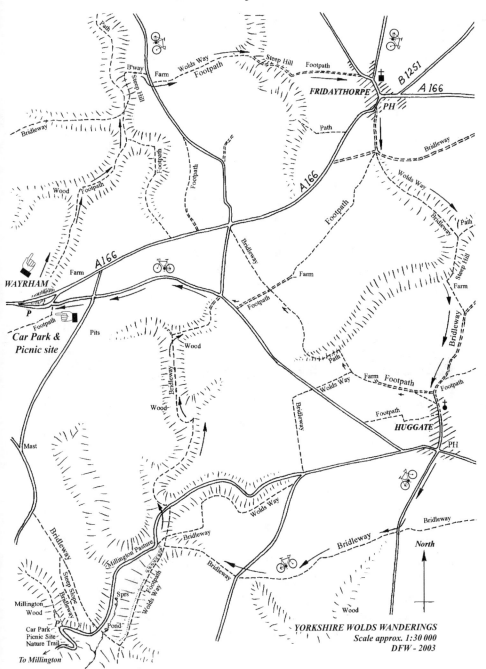

Map No. 15. Fridaythorpe and Huggate area

the Huggate area, while the path to the south-west leads to Huggate Wold House and a shorter route back to the car.

Taking the bridleway down Holm Dale towards Huggate village. After a little over 1km you start to ascend passing close to Northfield Farm, (you can use either path as shown on the map). You have now only 1km to walk southwards to reach Huggate. Again a further path to the right passing by Glebe Farm gives you another alternative route back to your car. On the main route, continue through the village and further south along Mill Lane which is the road to Warter village. Just along the main road in Huggate is The Wolds Inn, a favourite haunt with many weekend walkers.

After 1km on the Warter road, take the bridleway to your the west which is a section of the Minster Way. This path takes you towards Millington Dale passing the quiet lane by Cobdale Cottage (north of Cobdale Farm). Continue west and start descending to join the Wolds Way footpath crossing from south to north. Head north whilst admiring the excellent view to your left, looking west along Millington Dale.

After dropping down to cross the road along Millington Dale, continue by the path over the road along the grassy dale called Frendal Dale. This

---

Fact File: Wayrham to Fridaythorpe and Huggate

Start/Finish: Wayrham Picnic Area. Grid ref: 835568. A half day walk with plenty of hills around the highest parts of the Wolds. Much of the northern section of this walk forms part of the Wolds Way.

Location: South side of A166, 5km west of Fridaythorpe.

Max. length of main walk: 20km (13 miles), typical time: 5 hours.

Length of shorter walk: 15km (10 miles), time 4 hours, (many options).

OS maps: Landranger 106, Pathfinder 666 (SE 85/95), Explorer 294. Shop & Pub in Fridaythorpe and Huggate villages.

Cycling: With so many quiet country lanes and bridleways around Huggate and Millington, good use of the OS map will identify a number of circular cycle rides, (though take care on some of the steep descents!).

path meanders northwards for 1km before entering the trees at Great Plantation. After another 1km the bridleway turns sharp right, (east), and steadily climbs out of the trees to meet the road junction close to East Greenwick Farm. Turn left and the short walk of 2km westwards takes you back to the picnic site and car park.

The total length of that walk is around 20km, but with so many paths crossing this part of the Wolds you have many options to customise the ramble to suite your preferred distance and the weather conditions. The quiet dales and wooded areas give you many opportunities to study the wealth of animal life and wild flowers in abundance.

Walk 15: THE WHARRAM PERCY AREA

Heading northwards from Fridaythorpe, it is only a few kilometres to Thixendale village in the North Riding. The dale beyond the village is in many respects very similar in appearance to Millington Pasture - steep sided with a narrow lane slowly winding along the flat valley bottom. Many of the lanes around this area of the Wolds make for excellent cycling, with various bridleways linking them together to form circular routes.

The main irritation in planning a circular route in this part of the Wolds is the fact that you are on the 'join' of all three OS maps covering the area, numbers: 100, 101 and 106, in the 1:50,000 Landranger Series. This minor annoyance should not stop you from enjoying the dales and villages on your travels, particularly the deserted medieval village of Wharram Percy, just to the west of the former railway line from Malton to Driffield. However, help is now at hand in the shape of the new OS Explorer series of maps, No. 300 covers the complete route in far greater detail.

The site of Wharram Percy is sign posted from the B1248 Malton to Beverley road, just to the south of the village of Wharram le Street and around 10km south-east of the towns of Norton and Malton. The lane, marked to Burdale, takes you the short distance to a car park just to the south of Bella Farm.

Just 1km from this car park, along the track to the west, the important medieval site can be found. Now, a quick look at most OS maps, particularly of the Wolds region will soon find you spotting many 'site of lost village' markings. However, Wharram Percy is an exceptional example and well worth a visit.

The Ruined Church at Wharram Percy

Over the past 40 years dedicated teams of archaeologists have painstakingly scratched away at the soil on these chalk dales to slowly reveal part of the history of this settlement, and with it, many aspects of how our forefathers eked out their living on the Wolds of Yorkshire. Throughout the dale, a succession of markers and information boards guide you around this area, indicating the locations of many dwellings from centuries ago.

With the eerie site of the derelict church of St Martin, without its roof and half of the tower collapsed, your guide posts tell you some of the history of Wharram Percy village. So often the size and development of the village church tells much of the story of a community: how large it grew, how wealthy it was, when it started to decline and how quickly. St Martin at Wharram Percy is a perfect example.

The first clues of a timber house of worship date back to 10th century. A stone building was erected the following century with further extensions in the 14th century. The church could then cater for a congregation of well over a hundred. The Black Death, changes in farming methods with the enclosure of fields and the call of industry in the developing towns and cities all contributed to a steady decline of the village. However the church lingered on and for many years the people from Thixendale village and the surrounding area made the long trek over the wild fields to worship at Wharram Percy. In 1870 the second Sir Tatton Sykes arranged for a village church (dedicated to St Mary) to be built in Thixendale, accelerating the demise of that at Wharram Percy.

Just to the east of the deserted village site, is the track bed of an old railway. The full story of the Malton and Driffield railway line running through this most difficult Wolds terrain is, even by the standards of the 'railway mania' period, quite remarkable. The original promoters of this little known railway were not so much trying to link the small market towns of Malton and Driffield, but rather, had grander ideas to provide a main line direct route between Newcastle and Hull. By linking with the scheme proposed by the Thirsk to Malton Railway, the plan was to short-cut the longer journey to Hull via Selby, and by 1860, via York.

The thinking may have been grandiose, but the planning and building of the railway was not. Far from being built as a main line railway with double tracks, few curves and low gradients, the Malton and Driffield promoters soon had their plans cut back to a single line railway meandering through

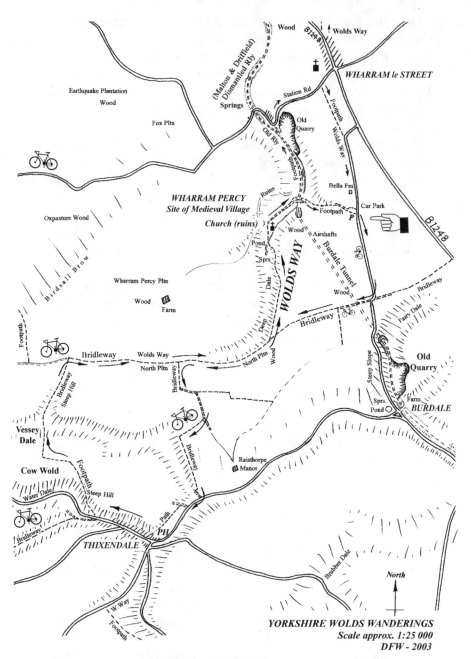

Map No. 16. Wharram area

the steep dales. Further, the junction with the Hull to Scarborough route, south of Driffield, resulted in trains from Malton facing northwards and thus preventing the efficient through-running of trains to Hull.

The line opened on 19th May 1853 and was immediately destined to become a struggling branch line throughout its existence. The stations were not logically positioned to serve the few villages that the line passed on its 30km from Malton to Driffield. It did however benefit the local farming economy and stimulate the growth of two large chalk quarries at Wharram and Burdale. It was nevertheless to be a very early casualty of closure, passenger services ceased in June 1950 and the local goods pick-up service stopped on 18th October 1958.

For a small independent company the building of the Malton and Driffield Railway over and through the Wolds was a massive undertaking. Burdale tunnel at just under a mile in length (1200m) cut through hard, difficult chalk. Having served royalty on occasions, when Sledmere and Fimber station was used en route to nearby Sledmere House, the quiet, unhurried railway slid quickly into the history books and oblivion.

Sledmere and Fimber station site, 4km south-west of Sledmere by the B1251 and B1248 roundabout, has been converted into a delightful picnic stop-over with car parking, toilets and childrens play ground. To the north the line of the former railway is still clearly visible for most of its length up to Burdale tunnel entrance, and again beyond the north portal of the tunnel amongst the trees, passing the deserted Wharram Percy village along to North Grimston and Settrington.

Leaving your transport in the car park south of Bella Farm, just on OS map number 101, a short circular walk can be enjoyed before investigating the site of Wharram Percy. So firstly, head south along the quite country lane towards Burdale for 1km. At the point where two right-angle bends occur in the road, a bridleway crosses the lane. Until a few years ago this formed part of the Wolds Way, though following a long campaign this has been re-routed to pass through the deserted village to the north west. Head west past the clump of trees, (which mark the line of Burdale tunnel beneath), and walk the short distance to North Plantation (now on OS Landranger map 100). Another footpath leads down the valley northwards to Wharram Percy, thus giving you one to two hours walking together with time spent exploring the ruins. For a longer ramble, stay on the bridleway heading west until a second small plantation is reached, also marked North

Plantation on the map. At the start of the trees turn south heading down the bridleway past Wold House and meandering down to the lane leading into Thixendale village, just 500m to the south-west.

Walking through the village you will see that there is both a welcoming public house and small shops where refreshments can be purchased. Walk right through the village towards the dale marked Water Dale on the map where you will be offered a choice of paths to your left and right. The left bridleway heads west past Thixendale Grange, however, take the footpath to the right heading northwards up the steeper hill over Cow Wold. This is again the Wolds Way and drops down into Vessey Pasture Dale before climbing again up to 220m then turning due east to take you back to North Plantation. This time, take the path north, dropping down into Deep Dale and the tranquil remains of Wharram Percy village.

You pass a series of springs which had been dammed by the medieval settlers to form ponds to provide water and keep fish stocks. The grave yard and St Martin's church beckon you to quietly look around and learn the history of the church, historical information is clearly set out on display panels inside the building. Back outside the church, a succession of information signs guide you around the site, pointing out the many dwelling houses that had been built, demolished and rebuilt, only to fall into decay over the centuries until just a slight mound of foundations remain.

Take care not to damage any remains of this site as it is classified as an ancient monument of important historical value. As you leave the location head eastward to the line of the former railway. The north portal of Burdale tunnel is just out of sight amongst the trees. The track bed to the north has been utilised to accommodate the footpath that ran along side the railway towards Wharram le Street village. This along with another large chalk quarry is around 1km to the north. Like the larger quarry at Burdale, this site is now also derelict. The car park is only 500m east of the railway track bed up the clearly marked track out of the dale.

All this area of the high wolds makes for excellent walking and cycling. Look at the maps for ideas on further circular walks and with most of the lanes around Thixendale being very quiet, a number of enjoyable cycle routes can be made linking bridleways to the roads. Not far from Thixendale is the country house at Birdsall, alongside the tidy estate village approximately 5km south of Norton.

Malton and Norton stand at each side of the River Derwent in North

The Heart of The Wolds

Yorkshire. The main A64 trunk road by-passed the towns in the late seventies, letting them breath again, though Malton can still often be a bottleneck for traffic heading north to Pickering and the moors. An array of shops and places to eat are located around Malton centre, along with a tourist information office open all the year.

Fact File: Wharram Area Walks

Start/Finish: Car park south of Bella Farm. Grid ref: SE 867644. A number of steep hills to climb on this high Wolds circular walk.

Max. length of main route: 13km (8 miles), typical time 3 to 5 hours.

Length of shorter ramble: 5km (3 miles), time 1.5 hours.

OS maps: Landranger 100 & 101, Pathfinder 656 (SE 86/96), Explorer 300. Pub & shop in Thixendale village.

Points of special interest: Medieval village of Wharram Percy, excellent walking on the high Wolds around Thixendale.

Tourist information: Office at 58 Market Place, Malton. Tel:(01653) 600048.

Cycling: The route described is a mixture of bridleways and footpaths, so you need to make a few diversions to give you a circular cycle route. With so many quite lanes around this part of the Wolds this can be easily achieved. I would suggest a route from the car park south down to Burdale, west to Thixendale village, then using bridleways or the lane through Water Dale, make your way towards Birdsall village. Turn east to Wharram le Street and back down to the car park, (note only footpaths give access to the medieval village site at Wharram Percy).

Chapter 7

EAST TO THE SEA

Walk 16: BURTON AGNES to KILHAM

To complete this hopefully appetite wetting excursion into the Yorkshire Wolds, this chapter turns to the east to follow the chalk hills to their rendezvous with the North Sea, where, like some giant unyielding fortress, the magnificent promontory of Flamborough Head stands resolute against the pounding of the tumultuous salty waves. But first, a more leisurely introduction to this part of the Wolds with some easy going rambles around the villages that cling to the southern edge.

To the west of Burton Agnes a pleasant 10km circular ramble can link you with the villages of Harpham, Lowthorpe, Kilham and Burton Agnes itself. It is an ideal route for those wanting a leisurely walk providing plenty of opportunities to stop off and enjoy a drink or two at the various public houses on the way.

A good starting point is at the picnic area located on an old loop of the A614 road (formerly A166), where there is plenty of space for car parking. Although all the route described is marked on OS map 101, it would be helpful to have the next sheet down (107), as the route is quite close to the join (or use Explorer 295).

The picnic site is located just off the main Driffield to Bridlington road, some 3km west of Burton Agnes and about 6km north east of Driffield. The actual site is by a bridge (known as Bracey Bridge) spanning a number of fresh water springs which form the source of Lowthorpe Beck. This stream flows south into Kelk Beck, then Frodingham Beck and eventually into the River Hull at a point close to the start of Driffield canal.

To start the walk, cross over the busy road and head northwards 2km into the village of Kilham where there is a shop and public house for a first refreshment stop. The map shows that there are a number of footpaths to the south side of the village around Beck Head. Leave the village heading east, crossing Haroham Lane and then walking in a straight line, south-east, to Burton Agnes just over 3km away. As described in the next chapter, the village is dominated by the splendour of Burton Agnes Hall, but also has a picturesque village pond, and public house and shop.

Whilst at Burton Agnes, mention must be made of the village of Rudston, 5km to the North. Although not included in this walk, Rudston is worth

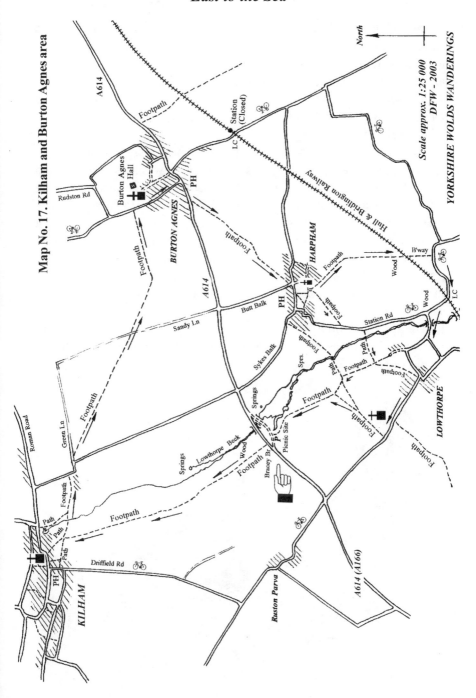

Map No. 17. Kilham and Burton Agnes area

YORKSHIRE WOLDS WANDERINGS

Scale approx. 1:25 000
DFW - 2003

visiting whilst you're in the area, especially if you are cycling which makes a detour straightforward. Of interest, in the grounds of All Saints Church at the side of the B1253, stands Rudston Monolith, a hugh standing stone almost 8m in height. It is believed to have been erected in the early Bronze Age, around 4,000 years ago, though no one really knows why. Also in this church yard is the grave of local writer Winifred Holtby, who wrote amongst other works, 'South Riding'.

After your stop at Burton Agnes, possibly including a visit to the hall, recommence walking along the main road to the west, take the footpath 1km south-west to the next village of Harpham, where the next welcoming village inn is to be found. A number of old earth works to the south of the village around the church suggest many changes in lifestyle in the area over the centuries and are worth a look. Three different footpaths head south and west out of the village allowing you to take your choice. One starts by the church and takes you south past Manor Farm and, crossing the railway twice, into Lowthorpe by Mill Lane. The next alternative also starts at the church in Harpham taking you via Station Road and then into Lowthorpe by Church Wood. The third path is from West End Farm in Harpham. It crosses the beck then turns to the north and back to the picnic site car park.

The Mallard Duck

It is only just over 1km from Lowthorpe back to the picnic site at Bracey Bridge, the complete walk being about 10km, depending on which route you take. There are only gentle slopes on this walk, but it can become rather muddy along some sections when the weather has been wet.

Fact File: Burton Agnes Area Walks

Start/finish: Bracey Bridge picnic site off main A614 - Grid ref: TA 077620.

A circular walk with easy slopes over rights of way through farm land.

Location: 6km towards Bridlington from Driffield.

Length of main walk: 10km (6 miles), typical time 3 hours.

OS maps: Landranger 101 & 107, Pathfinder 657, (TA 06/16), Explorer 295.

Several village pubs on route and small shops.

Tourist information office: Prince Street, Bridlington, Tel: (01262) 673474.

Special points of interest: Pleasant village churches and public houses along with the idyllic villages of Harpham & Lowthorpe. Burton Agnes Hall, described in the next chapter.

Cycling: Almost all this route is along footpaths and so unsuitable for cycles, however with the use of the many quiet country lanes in the area, a good circular cycle ride can take in many more of the villages. Try a route from Bracey Bridge to Langtoft, Kilham, Rudston then Boynton and down to Burton Agnes and Lowthorpe. A few good Wolds hills to get the leg muscles tingling!

Walk 17: FLAMBOROUGH HEAD and BEMPTON CLIFFS

Flamborough Head stands like a slender gleaming white beacon when viewed from the sandy beaches of Bridlington Bay to the south. Here, where the chalk Wolds sweep around to meet the North Sea this prominent headland has given stern resistance to the relentless waves over many thousands of years. The soft boulder clay to the south, around Bridlington Bay and along the length of the Holderness coast, has in stark contrast

Yorkshire Wolds Wanderings

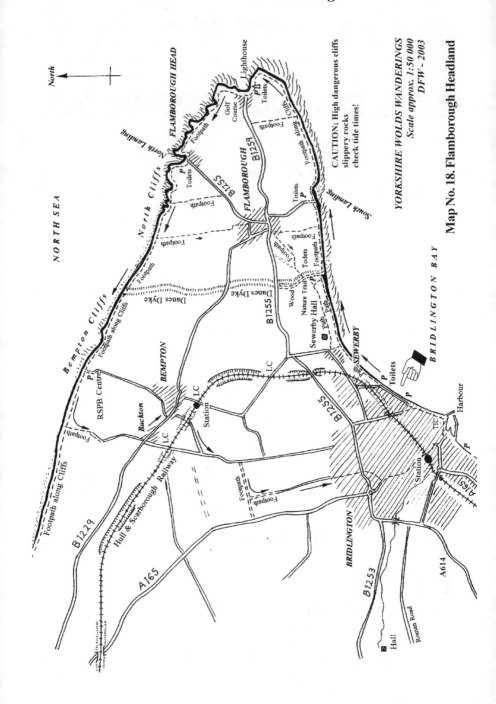

North

NORTH SEA

FLAMBOROUGH HEAD

North Landing

North Cliffs

B1255

Footpath

Golf Course

Lighthouse

P

Toilets

FLAMBOROUGH

B1259

Toilets

P

Footpath

Footpath along Cliffs

CAUTION: High dangerous cliffs
slippery rocks
check tide times!

Toilets

P

South Landing

Footpath

Footpath

Bempton Cliffs

Footpath along Cliffs

Danes Dyke

Danes Dyke

B1255

Footpath

Wood

Nature Trail

Toilets

P

Path Path

Sewerby Hall

SEWERBY

BRIDLINGTON BAY

RSPB Centre

P

BEMPTON

Buckton

LC

LC

Station

LC

LC

Footpath

Toilets

P

Harbour

TIC

P

Station

Hull & Scarborough Railway

B1229

A165

Footpath

Footpath

BRIDLINGTON

B1253

A614

Hall

Roman Road

A1253

YORKSHIRE WOLDS WANDERINGS
Scale approx. 1:50 000
DFW - 2003

Map No. 18. Flamborough Headland

100

been eroded away such that Bridlington itself is now around 8km west of the headland.

All around the main headland the cliffs are generally 40m in height capped with a grassy cap of boulder clay. Where the sea has permeated the white rock, many rugged coves, caves, rock arches and stacks have been created to form wonderland-like surroundings. Access to the rocky beaches and cliff faces can be made at North Landing, Selwick Bay by the lighthouse and South Landing. At each location there is ample car parking on the cliff top and numerous well established paths lead down to the waters edge.

Flamborough does get very busy with visitors in summer when the weather is fine but despite this the area is well worth visiting. An enjoyable and easy-going day can be spent wandering the many paths and exploring the rocky inlets and caves when the tide is safely out.

At the north side of the headland the cliffs of Speeton, Buckton and Bempton rise up to a very impressive 135m high, plunging almost vertically

The Puffin

into the sea. Not only is this spectacular coastal walking country, it is one of the most important breeding areas for many species of sea birds in Europe. Over the years considerable research has been under taken by ornithologists to protect the unique status of this stretch of coast line.

After many years of planning, an information centre and viewpoint has been established at Bempton Cliffs to enable the casual walker to learn and experience the extraordinary breeding patterns of many of the birds that visit this area and nest on the smallest of cliff ledges in colonies of thousands.

Spring time at Bempton sees the frantic activities of Gannets (at their only mainland breeding site in the country), Herring Gulls, Guillemots, Kittiwakes, Razorbills, Fulmars and, of course, Puffins. The Gannets and Fulmars will nest on the upper ledges of the cliffs, while the other breeds will seek out small crevices at locations throughout the cliffs.

Until quite recently it was considered acceptable for specialists to descend the cliffs on ropes to collect eggs for selling on to tourists. This is now viewed in a very different light indeed, with the true value of the locality now recognised through conservation. This area can be viewed as part of a coastal ramble, or accessed easily from a car park to the north of Bempton village located on the B1229, about 3km north west of Flamborough village.

Depending on your appetite for walking, you could consider a full day long trek, starting from Bridlington taking in the complete cliff top walk to Bempton, then returning to Bridlington by quiet country lanes. Alternatively various circular walks can be enjoyed around the headland using one of the car parks marked on the map to each side of Flamborough.

For this type of cliff top walking a few extra safety precautions are advisable. To enjoy the stunning views from your elevated perch, it should go without saying that a very windy day is not the safest occasion to be at the top of a 100m sheer drop to the rocky sea shore below! Great care must be taken when close to the cliff edge, including the grassy banks that steeply descend to the cliff edge. Young children with their boundless energy and inquisitive minds must be kept well clear of the obvious dangers. It would be wiser to save this walk for adults, with no more than a gentle sea breeze to avoid becoming a very unwelcome statistic of this beautiful but rugged coastline!

Another important factor is the tide. Many people meander away from

Flamborough Lighthouse

the idyllic coves to explore around the next headland only to find their exit quickly cut off by the incoming waves. If you want to scramble along the rocks and caves, check the tide times carefully, and leave yourself plenty of spare time to retreat to safety once the tide has turned.

The walk described covers the complete coastal trek from Bridlington, so if you prefer a shorter circuit, just pick up the route at the next car park. Since the arrival of the railway in 1846, Bridlington has been an established favourite with the holiday makers who enjoy its many miles of sandy beaches and harbour area. Unlike Scarborough, (its larger neighbour 25km to the north), it is not hilly and as such has a particular appeal to many types of visitor.

Start your day long walk from the northern end of the sea front. Leaving the promenade behind, head north eastward along the cliff top. Slowly height is gained and the Holderness coastline can be viewed to the south.

The parklands of Sewerby Hall are passed by after a few kilometres, then onto Danes Dyke where the cliff top perch is lost for a brief time. Danes Dyke is a massive defensive earthwork thought to have been constructed over two thousand years ago. Oddly, this is rather earlier than when the Danes came over to Britain in significant numbers, from the 9th century onwards, so the dyke's name is something of a misnomer. The dyke is almost 4km in length, up to 20m across and around 7m deep. The spoil from the trench was deposited at the eastern side to form a rampart around 5m high, thus forming a formidable defence to the headland. With the thick undergrowth of the passing centuries, the southern section is ideal for a pleasant 2km to 3km circular nature ramble from the car park.

Continuing our coastal trek, climb out of Danes Dyke back up to the cliff top and the 1.5km to South Landing. This is not unlike Danes Dyke in that you must again come down from your lofty position, only to climb back up at the other side. Flamborough village is only 1km north along the lane from South Landing. Back on the cliff top path you should be able to see the coast line on a clear day for over 30km southwards, along with the excellent panorama of Bridlington Bay to the west.

The next 3km to 4km brings you around the most easterly extremes of the headland, with the two lighthouses dominating the landward scene. The coast guard lookout station is passed along with the fog siren, before you turn to walk the short distance due west towards the main lighthouse (which is still in use). Built in 1806, the structure is 65.2m high and houses a 500 watt bulb which is magnified through prism lenses to create a 750,000 candle power light beam visible from over 30km out to sea. This structure replaces earlier octagonal lighthouse built out of chalk in 1674. It was recently renovated to make it safe for many more years and stands just inland of the present tower. A number of car parks and shops are located around the lighthouses.

The walk continues with a steady climb back up to the cliff tops and the 2km north-west to North Landing. Although not as high as the cliffs beyond Bempton, this is a very dramatic length of coast line with beautiful bays trapped between jagged headlands of white cliffs, peppered with thousands of Gulls on the many inaccessible ledges. Do not be tempted to stray off the established paths onto the steep grassy slopes of the cliff tops as they can be extremely slippery and dangerous.

The path lets you gently loose height as you approach the slipway in North Landing. This used to be the home of the RNLI Flamborough Lifeboat until it was recently decided to replace it with an inshore inflatable craft, much to the regret of many local fishermen. Back up on the cliff top a shop and cafe are positioned next to a very large car park and public toilets. The coastal path continues north westerly towards Bempton Cliffs and with a clear day, an excellent view around Filey Bay to Scarborough and beyond.

The cliffs now form a vertical wall of great height (135m), as it becomes the haven of so many sea birds. A number of areas have been fenced to allow you to watch the birds in safety. As with most coastal walks, this is an area to have the binoculars to hand. The maps shows you two different routes south, heading inland to Bempton village. The first one via a quiet country lane and the second, slightly longer route, by the path leading to Buckton, just 1km along the B1229 from Bempton.

You can now take the lanes south past the railway line towards Newsham Field. A track can take you off the lane, then south past The Grange to the outskirts of Bridlington and back to your transport. The complete walk is around 28km, so a full day could be enjoyed taking in the sea air, but study the OS maps and choose your preferred route. The main OS Landranger map is number 101, but the Pathfinder series number 646, (TA 26/27), is also a very useful sheet to have with you, covering the complete headland in great detail, as does the Explorer Sheet 301. For the fact file covering this walk see overleaf.

Fact File: Flamborough Head and Bempton Cliffs

Start/finish: Bridlington north beach - Grid ref: TA 194678, (or any of the car parks around Flamborough Head). A bracing trek along the cliff top for much of route, some short steep climbs up cliff steps.

Max. length of walk: 28km (17.5 miles), typical time: 7 hours plus for the complete route.

Length of shorter ramble: 9km (5.5 miles), up to 3 hours.

OS maps: Landranger 101, Pathfinder 646, (TA 26/27), Explorer 301.

Train and bus services available along route. Plenty of cafes, shops, pubs and public toilets along the route.

Tourist information offices: Bridlington tel: (01262) 673474, Filey tel: (01723) 512204.

Special points of interest: Sewerby Hall, Lighthouses, RSPB Bird Sanctuaries & view points, (remember to take your binoculars).

IMPORTANT CAUTION: High dangerous cliffs, not suitable for very young children or during stormy weather. Keep away from cliff edge and steep grassy banks which are very slippery when wet. Correct footwear is important and check the tide times if you want to walk along the beach.

Walk 18: FILEY BRIGG and SCARBOROUGH.

Although the seaside town of Filey is not actually on The Wolds, it does host the northern end of The Wolds Way long distance trail from the Humber Bridge. The town is midway between Flamborough Head and Scarborough, located in the bay of the same name, and south of the unusual headland called Filey Brigg. Unlike the bulk of Flamborough Head that is 5km wide, Filey Brigg is a narrow strip of rock jutting out just over 1km into the North Sea. It acts as the perfect breakwater to protect Filey Bay from the most severe pounding of a north-east gale. Spectacular waves are sent crashing over the rocky Brigg and into a mass of spray many metres above the angry North Sea.

East to the Sea

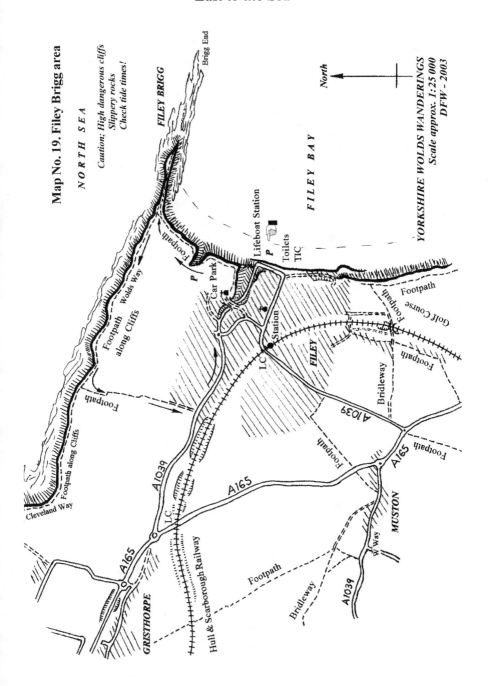

Map No. 19. Filey Brigg area

NORTH SEA

Caution; High dangerous cliffs
Slippery rocks
Check tide times!

FILEY BRIGG

Brigg End

FILEY BAY

North

YORKSHIRE WOLDS WANDERINGS
Scale approx. 1:25 000
DFW - 2003

Lifeboat Station

P

Toilets
TIC

Footpath

P

Car Park

Footpath   Wolds Way

Footpath
along Cliffs

Footpath

Footpath along Cliffs

Cleveland Way

Footpath

Station

L.C.

FILEY

Golf Course

Footpath

Bridleway

Footpath

A 1039

A165

Footpath

A1039

A165

Bridleway

MUSTON

W. Way

A1039

Footpath

Bridleway

A165

L.C.

Hull & Scarborough Railway

GRISTHORPE

The Wolds Way trail enters Filey from the west, with coastal paths coming from the north on the Cleveland Way, and the south from Bempton and Flamborough. Like the circular routes described in Walk 17, a short walk can be enjoyed from Filey town centre walking along the Brigg, then northwards before returning back along tracks to the town.

A number of car parks are located around Filey, with a large one to the north of the town ideal for this ramble along the coast. The circular walk is about 6km in length, leaving the car park by the cliff path northwards for 1km. You then follow the path along the narrowing brigg easterly for almost another 1km before a steep descent brings you down to the high water mark. If the tide is out you can walk with care almost 1km east along the rocks, taking care on the slippery surfaces.

Turning back, climb up onto the cliff top path again. On a clear day the views, south across Filey Bay to Bempton Cliffs and Flamborough Head, and, north to Clayton Bay and Scarborough can be memorable. As with the walk around Flamborough Head, this coastal trek will feel the full force of strong winds, so take extra care if the weather is inclement. You can walk around 2km along the coast with the cliffs rising to over 70m high before you come to a path leading southwards for 1km, then east back into Filey town. Naturally there are plenty of shops and facilities for walkers, and a tourist information centre near the sea front.

For a longer walk the coastal path can be followed northwards into Scarborough, a distance of just over 10km. You can make your return journey by train. The railway line from Hull to Scarborough seems to have a more certain future these days.

The line from Hull to Bridlington was opened in October, 1846. Most of the route passing through Beverley and Driffield was straight forward to construct as it passed over low flat countryside (though this did necessitate a large number of level crossings).

North of Bridlington, on the stretch to Seamer and Scarborough, the route took the line over the chalk Wolds, and took a further year to construct, with a large number of long chalk cuttings, embankments and steeper gradients. The complete railway between Hull and Scarborough opened on the 20th October, 1847. The northern section between Bridlington and Seamer Junction has been reduced to single line status although stations at Bempton, Hunmanby, Filey and Seamer are still open.

As the largest Yorkshire holiday resort, Scarborough has an array of attractions for the visitors. The Norman castle dominates the landscape standing atop of the headland which divides Scarborough's sandy beaches. From Scarborough, The Cleveland Way long distance footpath continues north up the coast, past Whitby and Saltburn, before turning inland to circle the North Yorkshire Moors.

The moors themselves create another excellent walking area and a magnet for ramblers. Several treks and cycle routes are featured in the author's book 'Yorkshire Railway Rambles, Volume One, North and East'. It includes most of the converted railway trails that have been developed over the past four decades throughout the area.

Fact File: Filey Brigg and Scarborough

Start/Finish: Sea Front by Lifeboat Station. Grid ref: TA 121808. A bracing circular cliff top walk, plus a scramble along the Brigg at low tide.

Location: North end of sea front in Filey Bay.

Max. length of walk: 7km (4 miles), typical time 2 hours.

Length of short ramble: 4km (2.5 miles), 1.5 hours.

OS maps: Landranger 101, Pathfinder 624 (TA 08/09/18), Explorer 301. Train & bus service to Filey Station. Good selection of pubs, shops & cafes in Filey town and Scarborough.

Tourist information office: Filey Tel: (01723) 512204.

Points of special interest: Excellent sea views from cliff tops.

IMPORTANT CAUTION: Like the Flamborough Head walk, Filey Brigg has high dangerous cliffs, not suitable for walking in stormy weather or with young children. Check the tide times and take special care if you want to walk to the end of the Brigg.

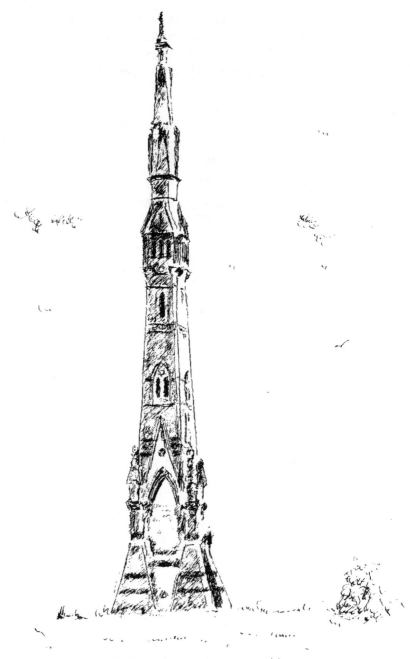

The Tatton Sykes Monument

Chapter 8

GREAT HOUSES of the NORTH WOLDS

To the south-west of Malton is the grand estate of Castle Howard. This magnificent house with its many acres of parkland is a well known attraction in the north of England, and can be easily found just off the A64 or B1257. Yet further to the east, and up onto the Wolds a number of smaller and less well known county houses still survive for the public to visit and marvel at the treasures they contain.

Sledmere House is the home of Sir Tatton Sykes, 8th Baronet. The present house dates from 1917 on the site of an 18th century house that was almost completely destroyed by fire in 1911. It is built in a similar style, though larger than the original building it replaced and is located at the south side of Sledmere village, 15km south-east of the town of Malton and 10km north-west of Driffield. The B1252, B1251 and B1253 roads all pass through the locality. Being an estate village built to house the employees of the mansion and surrounding farms it is all very neat tidy and of the same uniform architecture.

At each end of the main street stands a monument. The Eleanor Cross, to the west end of the village, was erected at the end of the 19th century and later adapted as a general war memorial after the Great War of 1914-1918. The Waggoner's memorial, standing further to the east along the main street, was erected specifically as a war memorial and dedicated to the men who formed the local 'Waggoners Regiment' and gave their lives fighting in the Great War.

The original house included the work of another Yorkshireman, Joseph Rose who, as one of the country's famous 18th century plasterers, was responsible for the decorations in many parts of the mansion.

A significant collection of furnishings in the Chippendale, French and Adam styles are on view to the visiting public. Fortunately, almost all the furnishings of the original house, along with drawings were salvaged in a very organised operation as the roof burned fiercely (from where the blaze started). Outside, the beautiful parklands were originally designed by Capability Brown, though it is thought that the Sykes family modified these plans appreciably, along with the walled rose garden.

Over the centuries the Sykes have provided the area with some very colourful characters to hold the title of Baronet. As the then largest land

Sledmere House

owners in East Yorkshire, they are credited with making great strides forward in the late 18th and early 19th centuries, converting many acres of barren Wolds fields into prime arable land. Their methods were soon copied by other farmers bringing both wealth and employment to the area.

Other members of the family have gained great respect, both for their work locally and nationally. It was Col. Sir Mark Sykes, who in 1912, whilst commanding a battalion of the Green Howards in the Territorial Force raised the private regiment known as the Waggoner's Reserve. This regiment consisted of more than 1,000 specialist waggoners from the many farms on the East Yorkshire Wolds. It was embodied at the outbreak of the Great War and sent to France, where they suffered severely in the retreats of 1914.

The house is open to the public at Easter and then from the beginning of May to the end of September. There is a restaurant, gift shop and a variable programme of exhibitions throughout the open season. To check on visiting times collect a leaflet from the tourist information offices, or telephone the house on 01377 236637.

Burton Agnes Hall. The village of Burton Agnes is located on the A614 (A166) between Driffield and Bridlington (see walk No. 16). The Hall, which is open to the public, is accredited to the work of Inigo Jones, and is visible to the north side of the main road through the village. This splendid late Elizabethan house and gardens are the home of the Cunliffe-Lister family, who are descendants of the original owners of Burton Agnes Hall four centuries ago.

Along with the many splendid rooms and galleries with their beautiful carvings, the house is noted for a collection of fine paintings by Gainsborough, Pissarro and Renoir. Four centuries of accumulating treasures plus the attractive gardens around the house, make this a most rewarding visit for the family.

Along with a cafe and a flower, herb and plant sales area, the house is open to the public from the beginning of April to the end of October.

Also located in the grounds are giant board games and the 'Riddle of the Maze' to keep the children and the young at heart amused. Local tourist offices will have the brochure, or telephone the house on 01262 490324.

Burton Agnes Hall

1km east of the nearby village of Rudston is on the B1253 is Thorpe Hall. Built in the early part of the 18th century with a large parkland to the south of the B1253 in the valley of the Gypsey Race river that flows easterly into Bridlington Bay.

Another 3km eastward along the B1253 brings you to the village of Boynton and Boynton Hall. Like Thorpe Hall it is located south of the main road in the Gypsey Race valley. A large manor house already stood on this site when it was purchased by William Strickland in 1649, but the present Hall took shape later that century, with many additions and alterations in the 1700s. The house remained in the Strickland family until 1951 when it passed to the Marriott family.

Both Thorpe Hall and Boynton Hall are private houses and are not open to the public, but there are a number of footpaths that run along the boundary of the parklands and southwards to the former Roman Road at Wold Gate. Campers and Caravanners can pitch in the camping ground located in the original walled garden of Thorpe Hall.

South of Wold Gate and around 1500m from Boynton Hall is Carnaby Temple, an octagonal folly built in 1770. Although the windows have been bricked up, the tower is a prominent land mark on the hill only 1km north from Carnaby village on the A614 (A166).

Sewerby Hall. Some 3km NE from Bridlington town centre, Sewerby Hall is located at the south side of the B1255. The parkland and Georgian house occupy a commanding cliff top position at the north side of the bay. Many of the rooms retain their original decorations from 1714 to 1720, when the house was built by John Grame. Over the years the grandson and great grandson of the builder have undertaken various extensions to the house, with two wings and a porch added around 1808 with further extensions in the 1820s. More work went on in the 1840s and 1850s until the house took the size as seen today.

The complete house and parklands were purchased by Bridlington Corporation in 1934. The 410 acres included two tenanted farms and four lodges along with extensive woodland. Over the years of being open to the public, various facilities have been added including an art gallery, fine tea rooms and restaurant, and an impressive display of mementoes dedicated to the pioneering aviator Amy Johnson. Born on 1st July 1903, in Hull, Amy Johnson was a remarkable woman. After studying for a B.A. at

Sewerby Hall

Sheffield University she moved down to London to work in the legal profession. In 1928 she joined the London Flying Club at Stag Lane Aerodrome. The following year she gained her pilot's 'A' licence, making her first solo flight after only 16 hours of tuition. Just five months later she became the first British woman to obtain her ground engineer's licence.

The next year she flew into the history books with her solo flight from England to Darwin in Australia, landing on the 24th May 1930. The flight, in a two year old Gypsy Moth costing just £600, took her nineteen days and made her an instant hero around the World. She continued to set many other records in the field of aviation before her tragic death in January 1941. She had joined the Air Transport Auxiliary during the second World War and died when her aircraft crashed into the Thames. Her body was never recovered. Her father presented the 'Amy Johnson Collection' of mementos and souvenirs to the Sewerby Hall Museum in 1958.

Outside the house in the acres of lovely parkland there is a walled garden, golf course, putting and bowling greens and a mini zoo. You can gain access to the grounds throughout the year, with the art gallery and museum inside the house open from April to October, with limited access through some of the winter months. Further information available from tourist offices or by telephoning 01262 401392.

A number of other East Riding houses that are open to the public include Burton Constable Hall. A fine Elizabethan house located near the village of Sproatley, to the north-east of Hull. It has many splendid collections of note and is sited in another beautiful parkland creation of Capability Brown. This house is covered in greater detail in Yorkshire Railway Rambles, 'The Hornsea Trail'.

To the west of the county Burnby Hall and gardens are near to Pocklington. This site is famous for the beautiful lakes that contain a national collection of water lilies and many varieties of fish.

South of the River Humber, 8km north of Scunthorpe and not too far from the Humber Bridge, is Normanby Hall, a fine Regency mansion, with parklands open to the public. Also on the south bank, Elsham Hall Country and Wildlife Park is only a few kilometres north east of Brigg and has many attractions including the animal farm and miniature zoo, along with nature walks in magnificent parklands.

Many other country houses add to the rich heritage of the area, surrounded by their mature parklands. In many cases the size of the park

The Deep visitor attraction in the heart of Hull

has been greatly reduced and turned over to farming, as the ever increasing costs of this labour intensive job of maintaining them proves prohibitive. Make good use the tourist information offices that keep plenty of details about houses open to the public, including all the opening times and information of any admittance charges.

Finally, visitors to the Yorkshire Wolds should not overlook a trip to the much revived city of Kingston upon Hull. With over a million passengers arriving and embarking through King George Dock continental ferry terminal, the city is getting quite a vibrant buzz from this increase in tourist trade. It has half a dozen interesting museums tucked into various corners of the old town area and city centre.

In High Street, in the old town area, is Wilberforce House. This house was the birthplace of anti-slavery campaigner William Wilberforce and now, as a museum, is open all year round. The adjoining building is the equally fascinating Street Life and Transport Museum, and only a little further along High Street is the Hull and East Riding Museum of Archaeology. Whilst in the old town area, visit Holy Trinity Church, the largest parish church in England dating from the 1300s. Hereabouts, just to the east of the River Hull and accessible by a new footbridge and cycle way, is the City's own outstanding Millennium Project; The Deep. This attraction gained instant international recognition as an exceptional visitor attraction, describing itself as a 'Submarium'. Since its opening in spring 2002, around a million visitors a year have been attracted to this landmark building located at the mouth of the River Hull. It really is a must for all age groups.

In the city centre, the Maritime Museum, housed in the old Town Dock Offices, covers many aspects of Hull's seafaring history along with fascinating details of the whaling fleet, a significant industry that has now completely vanished from the city. Just across Queen Victoria Square from the Maritime Museum is the recently extended Ferens Art Gallery, a Mecca for local art lovers. For further information about all of Kingston upon Hull's many visitor attractions, contact the always helpful tourist information centres, located in Queen Victoria Square and the Central Library in Albion Street, (tel: 01482 223559).

Whether you take the train, bus or car, or go under your own power on a pedal cycle, or don your walking boots, the Yorkshire Wolds has much to offer anyone who loves to wander the unspoilt countryside and discover all about its history and heritage. Appreciate this beautiful area of Britain, so often referred to by ramblers as England's best kept secret.

Above all else, enjoy your wanderings through the Yorkshire Wolds.

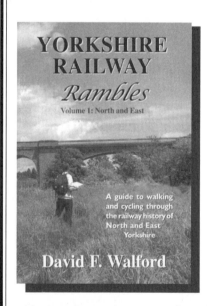